Mystery of MA's Ugly Pickle

By Martin Michael Neveroski

Marty and Carla

ISBN 978-0-9837506-1-1

First Printing, November 2011
Trade Paperback Edition

Printed in the United States of America
Writers Cramp Publishers
http://www.writerscramp.us/
editor@writerscramp.us

Chapter 1

The story starts back in the early twenties when as a mere fetus in my mother's womb, we were brought to America by my patriarchal Grandfather, Major Peter Barnoski. At the end of the First World War in 1919, many foreigners came to establish a home in what they believed was the 'land of plenty,' and becoming an American citizen was an automatic move to riches. What a 'crock' that turned out to be. Grandfather's plan was to start a business similar to the one he sold in Poland and bring Grandmother Sophie, his two daughters Helen and my ma, Francis, to join him later. With the sale of his thriving nursery business, plus being a retired Major in the elite Polish Army, he was already a moderately rich man. Grandmother Sophie was supposed to be the last one of the family to leave Poland and stayed to tie up any loose ends of the estate sale. One of the few things I still can recall of my grandfather is the sight of him in his wheelchair. He spent his last few years an invalid, because of a massive stroke. He believed and trusted so much in the progress of America, he kept his money in the local bank. When the banks folded during the stock market crash, he lost it all. It left him so devastated he never recovered. Some people as it turned out wisely kept their money secretively hidden, but not my grandfather.

He passed away when I was in my early years of elementary school. He was a very jolly man who was always buying me expensive toys. It is a shame the only thing I can remember about him now, is his huge roly-poly body pushing out the arms of the invalid chair. Although in his eighties, he still possessed a full head of white hair and a beard to match. His button nose and rosy cheeks made him a perfect candidate for a Santa Claus. He was never without his Meerschaum pipe that hung down from the corners of his mouth and an old hat that kept tumbling from his head as he nodded off to sleep. My ma and I were constantly replacing it and without looking up, his thank you would be a faint little grunt. His favorite time of day was when he fed the squirrels. My ma would load him down with unshelled peanuts and wheel him out on the front yard. He wanted the nuts hidden in all parts of his clothing; shirt pockets, pant cuffs and even the brim of the sweat-stained old felt hat.

We would stand on the porch and watch the anxious squirrels come scampering down the three elm trees that fronted our house. They came in droves from the cemetery across the street. It was hysterically funny seeing them frantically climbing over one another in their haste to get at those tasty peanuts. They must have numbered in the hundreds because at the height of their frantic search for the goodies, we could not see grandfather. He sat without moving a muscle in fear it would scare them away. When their onslaught was over, he nodded back to sleep and the hat would be lying on the ground by the wheelchair.

I will always remember the day we found him out in the yard with the pipe hanging from his mouth, and that old felt hat waiting for us to place back on his head for the last time.

Another thing was seeing him in the casket in our living room. At the time, I didn't know if it was a Polish tradition or if my ma couldn't afford a funeral parlor. For three days and nights, his body was on display. Neighbors and friends kept coming to pay their respects. The sweet-smelling flowers overwhelmed me when I walked in the room.

Each night before I went to bed, my ma had me kneel by the casket and say a prayer. I was to ask God to accept grandfather into heaven. She said God always hears the prayers of little children. I still remember how I stood and stared at his eyelids, hoping I could detect some movement. The biggest shock came when I got up enough nerve to reach up and touch his folded hands. It was not what I expected. They were hard and cold as stone. I was afraid my ma would want me to kiss him goodnight, but to my relief she never did. I was shocked and devastated as I watched his casket sinking into that deep dark grave. Real life came crashing down on my safe protected childhood. That was my grandfather's bio, a rich man from Poland who died a pauper in America, searching for the American dream.

Chapter 2

Our house was located on the corner of Barker Avenue and Cloud Street; a half-acre lot that was the last piece of real estate left of an old farm. The rest of the neighborhood housing was well established. Rumor was, the reason that the property stood idle for so long, a cemetery stood directly across the street. No one wanted to live that close to a bunch of tombstones and ghosts. In fact, all the other homes around the cemetery were at least two hundred feet from the Greenwood Cemetery fence. Ours stood less than one hundred.

Evidently, the graves and tombstones were of no concern to my militant grandfather and later on, for no one else in the family. We learned after living there awhile, we never paid any attention to the tombstones. For me, however, the cemetery would become a devastating experience and a very important part in my story.

The old farmhouse must have been exactly what grandfather was looking for. It was a large two-story frame building with three bedrooms, one downstairs off the dining room and two upstairs. The living room and front door faced Barker Avenue. To reach the back door you went from the kitchen through a small pantry, then a lean-to shed that was the laundry room. To go out to my ma's garden, you made a left turn under an eight-foot high wooden framed arbor of large purple grapes. My grandfather made sure there were bedrooms for everyone. My ma had the one directly above the dining room and my grandfather before his death, had the bedroom downstairs, off the dining room. I had one of the two upstairs bedrooms, and Aunt Helen, for a time, had the other one.

There was also a two-bedroom apartment next door, which made the building a duplex. My ma thought that at one time the farm hand and his family lived there.

A coal stove in the dining room heated the entire house. Its job was not only to warm the rooms on the ground floor, but its heat had to travel up the stairs into the bedrooms. To accomplish this, grandfather purchased one of the largest coal-burning stoves available. The Acme Brilliant Baseburner was the biggest and best stove the Sears Roebuck Company had to offer. It was a designer's dream adorned with heavy nickel-plated trim, including the double-swung mica doors on the front. Even the four curved legs were nickel-plated. The stove looked so beautiful it seemed out of place in its dated surroundings. The cast iron beauty stood along the north side of the dining room, about three feet out from an asbestos-protecting wall. My ma gave it the nickname, Old Lucifer. At times, it got so hot you would think the devil himself was stoking it. In the winter months, the dining room became unbearably hot, but in all the other rooms, the temperature was comfortable. I know it will be hard for you to believe this, but you could purchase the stove for less than forty dollars, delivered.

OLD LUCIFER

The most pleasant room in the house was the bedroom directly above the dining room. I had that room when my ma took over grandfather's room downstairs. Old Lucifer's heat would rise up the open staircase, past a spindled railing that served as the east wall, then fill my bedroom. It kept me warm through most of the night, but before dawn, Lucifer had burned himself out. His wrought iron belly that was once glowing red-hot would be back to a cold black. Insulation as we know it today was not available back then and getting up on winter mornings was a very unpleasant experience. What they used for insulation on most of the houses, were sheets of newspaper under the siding. It did a poor job of keeping the cold out and made the building a firetrap.

It was a good thing that every one of our bedrooms had a feather bed; a large puffy comforter filled with goose-down. I swear if it was sub-zero outside, you stayed cozy warm under those wonderful feathers.

My ma was the one who kept Old Lucifer fired up and she was an expert at banking the coals so they burned slowly and lasted almost through the entire night. In the morning however, the fire was just ashes. It was a wonderful sound in the cold morning to hear her stoking the fire. I stayed under my feather bed until the heat rose up the stairs to warm my room once again. I felt sorry for my ma because she had to lug buckets of coal everyday from a barn more than 150 feet from the house. The colder the temperature, the more trips she had to make. I wanted to help, but I was too young and didn't have the strength to even lift a bucket filled with coal, let alone carry it.

The basement was not full-sized like most houses of today. Squeaky wooden stairs extending down from the dining room lead to the fruit cellar. The dimensions of the fruit cellar were ten feet by ten feet. The floor consisted of badly laid brick, which caused many stubbed toes. The walls were concrete scarred with long cracks running in every direction. They looked dangerously close to caving in at any minute. The ceiling was unfinished and only a little over five feet high. If anyone were taller than that, the person would have to bend at the waist to keep from bumping their heads on the floor joists. When my ma went down there, which was seldom, she could move around standing straight up. The cellar had another way down and that was on the outside of the building, where slanting doors swung up and out, but because of the eroding steps, we seldom used that entrance. The doors however, were great for sliding down in the winter months. Even though the cellar was in such bad shape, it was an important part of the house. In spite of the damp musty smell and the cobwebs, it stayed cool throughout the hot days of summer. My ma used it almost exclusively for storing all of her canned foods and perishable items. Besides the shelves that lined the outer walls, a special island rack stood in the middle of the room. She did a lot of canning and had her own system for labeling the jars. She preserved everything from her garden, including the yield from the fruit trees. The jars for everyday consumption lined the outer walls and her special items were on the island rack.

Each year she entered her canned vegetables in a contest at the County Fair. The judges sampled all the entries and awarded blue ribbons for first place. My ma won every year, especially for her canned pickles. She would label those jars, COUNTY FAIR ONLY and place them on the island shelf away from the others.

When she planned a meal, my job was to fetch anything she needed. If there was ever an errand I hated, it was going down into that cellar. It was not because of the dimly lit, cold damp smelling dungeon, but the fear of an enormous-sized rat that made our cellar his kingdom. It was a Norway rat. Its length can go over ten inches from its head to the base of the tail. It reached America by ship from Asia. It had been an economic and health problem since its arrival. That damn rat ate everything, vegetable or animal, dead or alive and had a ferocious temper. My ma named him Diabel, which is Polish for Devil. We never saw any other rat or mouse around our property. Diabel chased them away or killed and devoured them. We sometimes found tails of rodents lying on the cellar floor. I guess that was the only part Diabel didn't find appetizing. We never could catch him in a trap or get him to eat anything laced with poison.

A helpful neighbor tried to catch him and came frantically back up the stairs, two steps at a time. He was white as a sheet and you could hear the thumping of his heart. When my ma asked what happened he said, "I had him cornered but that crazy wild thing stood up on his hind legs, defying me to hit him. When I saw his eyes turning red and displaying those sharp fangs, I dropped the broom and got the hell out of there."

Whenever I went down in the cellar, I made enough noise so that Diabel knew someone was coming and had time to go to his secret hiding place. That way he would not have to defend himself by a surprise visit. We never discovered his hiding place.

In case you're wondering why we called him a Norway rat if Diabel came from Asia? I will save you asking that question… I have often wondered about that myself and have no idea.

Chapter 3

There is an old saying that goes like this..."If you want to make a gypsy fortune-teller laugh, tell her your future plans."

Well, my grandfather succeeded in fulfilling some of his plans for the future. He made the transition to America and bought property to start up a business that would also include a home for his family. His two daughters Helen and Francis made the trip, but not his wife Grandmother Sophie. She never made it to America. She died suddenly and unexpectedly. She had been suffering for many years with terrible head pains. The doctor wrote them off as acute headaches. Aunt Helen however, was a little skeptical of that diagnosis, especially after hearing grandma claiming she had seen God. She was a very religious woman and lived by the Bible, but never before had gone so far as to say God was actually visiting her. The doctor believed that grandma's sudden death was heart failure. To make sure the doctor's diagnosis was correct Aunt Helen requested an autopsy. When the report came back from the coroner, it stated that a large malignant tumor had formed on her brain and she had died from a stroke.

The two daughter's trip to America had to wait until after the funeral. They stayed to fulfill grandma's wish to rest alongside her parents in her beloved Poland.

My Aunt Helen was four years older and four inches taller than my ma Francis, who was barely five feet. Their height was the only feature that was different. If it was not for that, they could almost pass as twins. Aunt Helen was more feminine than my ma, who I would consider more tomboyish. They were both brown-haired beauties with hazel eyes and cute pug noses. Their complexions were flawless and never needed rouge for that healthy glow. The likeness even carried over to the fact that when they smiled or laughed, a dimple would appear in the same spot on their left cheek. Friends used to kid my ma by saying she was so stubborn she would not leave the womb until four years after Helen. There was one feature that was different and nature had nothing to do with it. My ma had a little scar above the temple caused by a fall from a tree; but it did not show under her hairline.

The only noticeable difference between my Aunt Helen and my ma were their opposite personalities. Aunt Helen had that extroverted self-assurance. My ma was more introverted and religious.

Grandfather wanted to find his girls a husband as soon as possible, so they could get started raising a family. He spent a lot of his time at Stash's tavern a few blocks up Barker Avenue. He thought it was a good place to spread the news that there would soon be two single daughters from Poland looking for husbands. This opened a few eyes knowing that the prospective husbands would be marrying into a financially sound family. There were many young men that came to the house, making their availability known. Many didn't fit my grandfather's requirements. I guess in Poland, the father always screened suitors first.

Aunt Helen had a mind of her own and didn't like my grandfather's effort to find a mate. She kept turning down the would-be-wooers saying that they all had dollar signs in their eyes. It wasn't that Aunt Helen didn't have an interest in raising a family; on the contrary, she planned to have at least four kids. In Warsaw, she spent many hours at hospitals and orphanages helping with the care of crippled children. She stated when the time came she would find the right man on her own. As it turned out, it only took a couple of months for Aunt Helen to accomplish it.

It happened when she joined the church choir and met Steven Jerome Waite. Aunt Helen had a beautiful alto voice and was a featured soloist at her church in Poland. Steve sang bass, which seemed rather strange coming from his tall beanpole body. The sight of his large black-rimmed glasses supported on the tip of his long narrow nose, gave the impression he was a nerd. The saying that 'looks can be deceiving' was certainly true for my Uncle Steve. He became my Uncle when he and Aunt Helen said their wedding vows on a beautiful Saturday morning in June. It was a quiet event with just a few friends; Aunt Helen wanted it that way. She said they would have a honeymoon when they could afford it.

I learned later that Waite was the English translation of Steve's Polish name, which I won't even try to spell or pronounce. Uncle Steve was in his late twenties and exceptionally good with numbers. In fact, he had just finished taking a correspondence course in certified public accounting. We used to test him at our family gatherings by giving him a list of numbers to add, subtract, multiply and then divide. We figured the answers on paper first and then without the use of pencil or paper, he had to come up with the total in his head. We could never stump him and the speed in which he came up with the answer was amazing. My Aunt and Uncle planned to have children, but something was wrong in their body chemistry; Aunt Helen couldn't conceive. They went to many doctors and took all the tests, but to no avail. They thought about adopting, but new and promising findings on the subject made them wait with the hope of raising their own flesh and blood. I grew up loving my Aunt Helen almost as much as my ma and I know that she thought the same about me. She was always chiding my ma with the statement; any time you want to give Michael to me, I will take him. My ma would counter with, "Don't hold your breath, Helen."

Chapter 4

I was born on November 15, 1923, the son of Mr. and Mrs. Martin Michael Neveroski, father deceased. My ma and Martin were married only a few months when he got his orders to go to the front lines for one of the never-ending skirmishes in the section of Germany, called Prussia. Lieutenant Neveroski died in a heroic attempt to save his comrades trapped in an ambush. They shipped his medals to my ma and she kept them on display, along with my grandfather's in the dining room china closet. The loss of my father Michael and my birth on the way, made my grandfather more determined than ever to have his first grandchild born on American soil. He believed the birth of a baby and starting a new life in a wonderful country would make it easier for my ma to get over her tragic loss.

Aunt Helen told me it was not easy for my ma to get over that loss. She and Michael were childhood sweethearts and after one more year in the Polish army, they were planning to join the exodus to America.

My grandfather firmly believed babies should be born in the family home. With the aid of a neighbor-lady, known as a mid-wife and Aunt Helen who assisted, said I was an easy delivery. My ma was happy I was a boy, so she could name me after my father.

My baptismal name was Martin Michael Neveroski, which made me a junior. My ma called me Januscheck, which in Polish means junior. That is how it sounded to me. I think in my ma's Polish, it meant junior. I have no recollection of my baby years. Things that happened before I was five, I learned about as I was growing up. For example, I almost died from a case of diphtheria, an acute, contagious disease that attacked little children and in most cases was fatal. It hit our town in epidemic proportions. My ma told me I had double diphtheria. I never knew if she meant twice as bad, or that I had it more than once. I think she meant the latter. Whichever the case, I was a very exceptional baby to have survived. She also tells the story of the time when she and our neighbor lady were driving to Laporte, Indiana, to do some business at the county courthouse. I was in the back seat with her little girl, Mildred who was also three years old. I guess we were kissing and hugging all the way to the courthouse and back, a total of twenty-two miles. Our mothers thought our kissing was just innocent fun and got a big laugh out of it. Two days later, they stopped laughing when my back seat lover and I came down with a bad case of measles. They never found out who contaminated whom.

I do remember the fifth year of my life when my ma left me for the first time. She took me to kindergarten and told me she would have to leave me there until after school. The thought of being without her was quite traumatic. I am sure the teacher understood how I felt, and had faced that situation many times. Taking me by the hand, she led me over to the class. "Children, this is our new classmate, Michael." They were sitting in a circle on the floor and in unison they all said, "Hi, Michael." Two of the kids immediately moved apart and signaled me to come and sit between them. I didn't know what they were doing on the floor until a ball came rolling to me. The teacher said, "Now, you roll it to whomever you would like to, Michael." We sat there playing roll the ball back and forth and it seemed like all the kids wanted to roll it to me. I think they saw how uncomfortable I was and wanted to make me feel welcomed. Well, their friendliness certainly helped, because it didn't take long until I had completely forgotten that my ma had left.

From that day on, I proudly walked the eight blocks all by myself to the Marsh Elementary School. You probably noticed the teacher called me Michael. My ma wanted me to use me middle name and I never questioned her.

Chapter 5

As I look back on my childhood, I can see that the great love and devotion for my mother, who I always referred to as my ma, was a big factor in shaping my entire future. A love that was so deep, I would have given my life to protect her from any harm. I realize most boys feel the same way about their mothers, but my feelings bordered on the brink of obsession. For instance, I once heard girls jumping rope to the timing of the chant...'step on a crack and break your mother's back' . . .'step on a crack and break your mother's back.' Many years after hearing that chant, I couldn't walk on a sidewalk without timing my stride to miss a crack. I never told anyone why I was walking that way for fear the other kids would laugh at me. When they asked, I told them I was practicing Hopscotch.

Then there was the time I heard, "if you see a falling star," it means someone in your family was going to die. I know it sounds silly, but every time I saw one fall, I immediately said three Hail Mary's and one Our Father, in hopes that my ma wasn't on God's list. There was one night in the fall of the year when the meteors were very active. They put on such a display; I quit playing outside and went into the house. There were so many falling stars it became impossible to keep up with the Hail Mary's and Our Fathers. How long it took me to grow out of those beliefs, I can't recall, but they ruled most of my adolescent years. My ma's teachings about God, the Bible and the Catholic religion were the most indelible of all. Aunt Helen told me her mother Sophie started teaching her and my ma about religion at a very early age and as it turned out, Helen believed that my ma was more like Grandmother Sophie than she was.

My ma read and quoted from the Bible and lived her life obeying the Ten Commandments. She made sure I also knew them by heart. Now and then, she would test my memory by stating a number and I would have to recite that commandment. Even though I had my doubts, I never let my ma know. For example when reading about how the world began, I noticed the picture of Adam and Eve didn't fit the story of their creation. My ma's Bible had a picture showing the Garden of Eden with Adam and Eve lounging peacefully among the wild animals. The question I wanted to ask my ma was...if Adam and Eve were the only humans on earth, why did they have to cover their private parts? I could see the animals weren't covering theirs.

The artist must not have read the bible or the story of life. I could understand not depicting their private parts, but why would Adam and Eve each have a belly button when they never had umbilical cords?

My ma was very strict about my private parts and taught me to refer to mine as a... 'peecha,' which is Polish for penis. It sounded to me like she was saying, 'peepka' and that is how I always said it. My peepka was to be touched only when washing it or going pee-pee. It was a sin to play with it at other times. If she said it was a sin, then it was so. I tried very hard to follow her wishes, which became very difficult to do, because my peepka was the tenderest part on my adolescent body and soon as I was naked, my hand automatically reached for it.

I don't remember at what age it started, but as I grew up an aching pressure would develop in my groin area. I felt if I could only squeeze my peepka awhile, maybe then the ache would go away. I fought the temptation at first, but as time went on it became more and more unbearable.

I got the idea that if I shoved my peepka between my legs, I could squeeze it with my thighs and by positioning it through my clothing, I wouldn't be touching it or playing with it. Following up on my idea, I arranged my peepka and squeezed as hard as I could. It brought relief immediately. This technique was the answer to my problem, because it didn't take long, and I felt some relieving contractions happening down below and the aching stopped. I hadn't reached puberty yet, so the contractions never produced any wetness. I was proud of myself for finding a way to ease my urges without going against my ma's wishes. I never touched my peepka with my hands and therefore I convinced myself that if I wasn't playing with it...then there was no sin.

My ma also warned me about women that lived sinful lives, girls who lure men into doing naughty things and sinning. She had a name for them...'Shoestring.' To this day, I never figured out the connection between a bad girl and a 'Shoestring,' but to her, it was the lowest kind of female on earth. I promised myself I would never have anything to do with a 'Shoestring'. I carried her warning throughout my entire life. History has proven there were many men sorry they ever...tied the knot with a 'Shoestring'.

I am sorry for the play on words... I just couldn't resist it. Oh, by the way, I found so many versions of the Ten Commandments I don't think Moses even got it right.

Chapter 6

Finding a husband for Aunt Helen was a lot easier than one for my ma. Helen had never married before and didn't already have a child for any young prospect to take into consideration. I think that was the reason so many eligible bachelors never made a proposal to marry my ma.

Five years had gone by since Aunt Helen and Uncle Steve said their vows, Aunt Helen said my ma was getting worried that marriage would never happen to her and I would grow up without having father-to-son guidance. She said my heroic father, Martin, talked on and on about all the things he would do if his baby was a boy. She feared that if her new husband wanted children of his own, her bearing years were passing by. With that possibility my grandfather in his anxiety, made my ma rush to accept the first real offer that came along.

It was a sailor named Frank Dramski. He was in his middle thirties, six feet tall with wide shoulders that tapered down to a small waistline. These features along with his dark wavy hair and handsome face had my Aunt Helen questioning why at his age and looks, some woman hadn't already lassoed him. She also thought it was strange that he would be interested in a widow with a five-year-old child. She warned my ma not to rush into any more thoughts about Frank, until we could find out something about his past. She said he had a questionable habit of not looking at you when he spoke. She said that was a sign of a liar. He had dollar signs in his eyes big and clear.

What they found out came from Frank himself. He said he had

been a sailor since he left his home in Poland as a teenager. He talked about the fact that he had sailed all over the world working for many shipping lines. Aunt Helen asked him to name one of them, thinking she could write to the company for some background. It seemed Frank didn't want anyone snooping into his past. He said that was his personal life and it should be respected. That should have raised a red flag at that statement. He said he heard about this port city that was growing rapidly and wanted to be part of it. The shipping business coming and going to Chicago and lumber from the mills in the state of Michigan made our new harbor the Mecca of job opportunities. He thought he would start by taking a job working on one of the tugboats. The fish were so plentiful they were rushing out to their nets two or three times a day and needed experienced sailors. The net profit for one company alone ran as high as $40,000 a year, which was astronomical considering the monetary situation at that time. Frank said the fishing industry was something he would be interested in and even planned on having tugs of his own.

I bet the gypsy fortune-teller would have really laughed at that plan.

Chapter 7

Frank wanted a quick marriage by a justice of the peace, but my ma wanted a church wedding held at St. Stanislaus. They both kept holding out until Frank threatened to back out of the whole idea. That is when my grandfather stepped in and had a long talk with Frank. Whatever my grandfather told him changed his mind and Frank agreed to the church wedding with one stipulation. It would have to be a small quiet wedding with no big celebration party afterwards. Frank said the reason he wanted a quiet ceremony was that he didn't have a dress suit to his name. Uncle Steve being about the same height as Frank lent him one of his, along with the shirt, shoes, socks and tie. Grandfather treated our small party to a champagne dinner at the famous Spaulding Hotel on Franklin St.

When Frank showed up to move in, all he brought with him was the borrowed suit and a sailor's duffel bag bulging with dirty work clothes. Right behind him at his heels was a large black tomcat. He never said anything about having a pet and later we found out why. Frank never considered the cat his pet. It was in his duffel bag when released from his job on a freighter in Rio de Janeiro. He found the kitten hidden in the duffel bag by the mother cat. Most ships had a cat on board to rid the rodents that infested the food supply. Frank said other cats would hide their babies to protect them from sailors who threw them overboard. He said he thought about getting rid of the cat many times, but good fortune kept coming his way and he came to believe that the cat was good luck and didn't dare part with it. He named the cat Dupa, which in Polish means ass, or your rear end. If you called someone a dupa in anger, it meant asshole. He never told us why he named the cat Dupa. Frank never petted the cat or for that matter showed any affection toward it at all. However, when he came

home, Dupa would run up and start rubbing his body against Frank's leg, purring with affection. Everyone agreed Dupa was the largest cat they had ever seen. With jet-black fur, small round ears and green penetrating eyes that glowed in the dark, it led us to wonder if a Brazilian panther sired his mother. Dupa never touched any of the food my ma put out for him, but preferred to capture his own prey. After hunting all night in the cemetery, we would see him dragging rabbits, ground hogs, squirrels, birds and sometimes even the remains of another cat back to the house. He was a ferocious hunter and didn't show affection for anyone but Frank, which was certainly all right with the rest of us, because we didn't pay much attention to the cat either. The only time Frank ever did, was when he came home in his usual bad mood and became irritated from the cats rubbing and purring, He would put his foot under Dupa's belly and fling him twisting and turning high in the air, but that crazy cat would always land on his paws with a loud screech. After a few stunned moments, he would start licking his sleek black coat and stare back at Frank as if to say... you are the asshole, not me. Dupa didn't hold a grudge very long however and was back between Frank's legs purring out love for his heartless owner.

One time Frank tried sending Dupa down to get rid of the rat

Diabel. The cat was all excited and anxious to hunt this new territory. When Frank opened the cellar door, Dupa charged down the steps with a screeching m-e-e-o-w. Frank closed the door so the rat couldn't use that route for his escape. It only took a few minutes before we heard the high screeching sounds of animals in battle. When the noises stopped, Frank opened the door for Dupa to come out. It took a little while, but when he did, he was limping on one leg and blood was running from his ear. That was the last time Frank could ever get Dupa to challenge Diabel. He tried to boot him down the stairs, many times, but Dupa would come bounding back out of the cellar before Frank could slam the door behind him.

Chapter 8

Less than a year after my ma and Frank were married, a devastating event changed America dramatically. It was the stock market crash on October 19, 1929. They named it *Black Tuesday*. When I came downstairs that morning, I was too young to understand the great tragedy that was taking place. Grandfather was yelling and screaming over the phone, my ma and Aunt Helen had their ears glued to the radio and Uncle Steve was jotting down numbers that my grandfather's ticker-tape machine was printing. All I could gather was something about a stock market crashing and banks all over America were claiming bankruptcy. My grandfather had his money in one of the four thousand that locked their doors. He also invested heavily in the stock market. There was great panic from coast to coast, as fortunes were being lost. People were committing suicide by jumping out of windows and they found others in their offices with self-inflicted gunshot wounds. The rich turned poor and my grandfather was one of them. He also became an invalid from a massive stroke.

It was a new world for the occupants on Barker Avenue. That Black Tuesday made each one of us try to find ways to bring money into the household. With the terrible depression that followed, that task wasn't easy to accomplish.

Many establishments went under and jobs as they used to say were 'scarce as hen's teeth.' It was almost impossible for me at my age to make any substantial wages. I tried getting a paper route, but I wasn't old enough and paperboys weren't giving up their route. I did the best I could by delivering advertising flyers on foot, door to door for a 'Ma and Pa' type grocery store. There were fifty flyers at one cent apiece. My pay was a whopping fifty cents! I know it doesn't sound like much, but a quart of milk was only fifteen cents and delivered right to your doorstep.

Uncle Steve, who was now a certified public accountant, did some absentee work for the city. It wasn't a steady income, but what little he earned helped. My Aunt Helen found employment at Stash's saloon, two blocks west on Barker Avenue. She worked there as an extra waitress on weekends. It was one of over two hundred saloons. There were so many beer parlors per capita; we called our town, 'Little Milwaukee.' It was surprising to Aunt Helen that people without jobs still had money for booze, but were very conservative when it came to tipping.

The wages Frank made at the fish company seldom reached home. His habit depleted his wallet. He, like the sailors of old, loved his rum. By the time he arrived, most of the bars in town had some part of his paycheck. There was one bar however he made sure he never showed his face on Friday nights and that was the one Aunt Helen worked at. She later learned he only frequented Stash's bar the nights she wasn't working. She was finding out a lot about Frank's clandestine behavior from her customers. There is a saying, 'a sailor has a girl in every port.' Frank it seemed had one in every neighborhood. Evidently, he didn't think the commandment, 'thou shalt not commit adultery,' applied to him. Aunt Helen's request for a background on Frank was still a good idea and his claim that Dupa was a good luck charm, wasn't working for our family.

Chapter 9

R ealizing that we had to fend for ourselves, my ma virtually rolled up her sleeves and immediately as they say, 'grabbed the bull by the horns.' To me she was an enigma. The many things she knew how to do and do them so well were completely baffling. We were surprised when she started her wallpaper-hanging business and became so proficient at it. The Breskin wallpaper and paint store downtown, soon referred customers her way.

What helped finance the business was some odd change grandfather kept in his bedroom. It was a pillowcase filled with silver dollars. I don't know how many coins he had, but at the age of four, he could completely cover me from head to toe. My ma said he liked to show off his loose change as he called it. He may have been able to flaunt the money back then, but in today's drug crazed world, it would have probably cost him his life, a lot sooner.

With that money, she purchased stepladders, planks and all the other necessary tools. Her transportation was my grandfather's brand-new 1928 Ford sedan, which cost him $585.00 cash.

If the house she was papering was anywhere near my route home from school, I would stop to help her clean up and load the car. Before we left, she liked to show her finished product challenging me to see if I could find where the seams of the paper joined. If the paper was still wet from the paste, maybe I could, but when it had dried, it was almost impossible. Her work was that good.

My ma was also a very good seamstress and started a business of making and renting out costumes for gala parties and balls. The busiest time was Halloween and New Years. Her creations won many prizes for the customers. Rent for the costume was $5.00 and after the event, they had to return it. Sometimes it would take weeks to track down the people to get the costume back. Many times the costumes were torn or stained. My ma never charged a damage deposit for fear of losing the rental.

Along with the time consuming job of homemaker and mother, she also found time to create and maintain the most beautiful yard and garden imaginable. My ma's flowerbeds were so gorgeous and artistically arranged, the city's newspaper sent out a photographer to take pictures to be in the color section of our Sunday paper. Her vegetable garden was also a thing to behold. It was back of the flowers among the fruit trees. In addition, an arbor was loaded with purple grapes. Whenever anyone asked what she grew, I would answer, "everything under the sun." The tomatoes looked like the ones you see in the magazine ads. My favorite treat in the morning was going out in the garden with a saltshaker and eat three or four tomatoes for breakfast. The pickles grew to award winning specimens. It seemed everything she planted flourished. The yield from the fruit trees each year was so plentiful, what she didn't use for canning, she shared with our neighbors. There was a cherry, peach and pear, along with four different varieties of apple trees. She had her own system of fertilizing them. Whenever we went fishing off the

Government pier and our catch was more than we needed, she would invite the neighbors over to clean some fish for themselves. The sharing of the fish was reciprocal and there were times they invited us. We dumped the fish into a large washtub of fresh water and everyone sat around cleaning what they needed. Although the neighbors were a mixture of German, Poles and Irish, we accepted the fact that we were all Americans now and got along just fine. There was a lot of wisecracking and laughter between us and I know it is hard to believe, but there were no fences separating our properties and doors never were locked, in fact I don't even remember a key.

After we cleaned the fish, we discarded the remains of over a hundred and some fish. My ma would dig around the trees; dump the water, fins, scales, guts and all, into those holes. She made sure she dug them deep enough so the smell of fish wouldn't attract animals. She always kept track of which tree had the last feeding. When people asked me why our trees had such healthy looking fruit, I would give them the most honest answer I could without divulging her secret. I would say, "If I told you the reason, you would think there was something fishy about it."

Some things my ma did, I didn't think she was capable of and that took place in the backyard area hidden from view. We raised chickens and ducks back there and it was my job to make sure they got plenty of feed and water. I couldn't give a name to any bird; because she said, it would then become a pet and not served at our kitchen table. When she planned a chicken dinner, I helped her catch it. We used a wire from a clothes hanger, straightened it out to about three feet and bent one end into a loop. When the chicken you wanted ran past, all you had to do was flip the wire underneath the bird and it would snag its leg. The ones that were destined for the chopping block were the ones that weren't producing eggs and she always knew which hen it was. The block was a stump from an old oak tree and it stood about three feet high. I couldn't believe how my ma, who was always kind to animals, could grab a chicken, chop off its head and fling the body on the ground. I was stunned watching it flip and turn until all movement stopped. I had the job of hosing off the block. There was another time she needed my help and that was the most devastating and shocking of all. It was when she planned to make duck-blood soup, a delicacy in Poland. She raised a beautiful white duck and it must have been just for this so-called delicacy. While sitting on a stool, she held the duck firmly trapped between her knees. Grabbing its bill, she bent it down against the duck's neck. She positioned the bird over a white porcelain bowl, and with her favorite culinary tool, the sword-breaker knife, she slit a deep gash across the top of the duck's head. Blood immediately spurted out and started dripping into the bowl. I watched the poor thing as it kicked and squirmed in its frantic effort to escape. It seemed like eternity for the last drop to pump out. When she finally released the duck's head, it hung down limply over the bowl of blood.

"Gee ma, why didn't you just chop off its head like the chicken, so the duck wouldn't suffer so long?"

She answered my question with, "The heart, Januscheck, has to keep pumping to make sure all the blood is drained." As soon as it was over, I ran to the toilet and threw up the tomatoes I had for breakfast that morning. I have never ever eaten Crew Plotna...duck-blood soup.

When she walked into the kitchen I asked, "How could you have done such a thing, ma?"

"Sometimes in life Januscheck, we have to do things like that to survive." At the time, I did not realize how that statement would haunt me later.

As I think about it now, I could have saved that bird from its horrible fate. All I had to do when I handed the duck to my ma was say, "He-e-e-e-e-r-s Donald!

Chapter 10

Two blocks west of my house on the corner of Barker Avenue and Tilden Street stood the area's neighborhood tavern, a two-story building, with living quarters on the second floor. The Wolinski family owned it for many years and passed it down to a member of the family. The owner of the bar at this time was Stanley Wolinski. Stanley immediately changed the business name from Wolinski's to just calling it, Stash's Tavern. Stash is short for Stanley, but pronounced as St-ah-sh. The Wolinksi's always made money in the liquor business even through the prohibition years. The eighteenth amendment to the constitution that made it unlawful to sell intoxicating liquor, was spirited by the prohibitionists or 'dry's' as they were called. The Wolinski's however survived by bootlegging and making their own 'bathtub gin.' They poured many drinks in their popular bar.

What also helped was the influx of those Poles, Germans, and the Irish who came from environments that considered drinking sophisticated and sociable. There was a rumor that the reason Wolinski's had never been raided, was under-the-table payments to the right people, but it was never proven. The tavern made a lot of money, but unlike my grandfather, the Wolinski's did not put their savings in a bank. Patrons believed that somewhere on the property was a Wolkinksi fortune. Through the years, thieves had ransacked the property, but never found a dime. The break-ins would happen whenever Stash would close the bar to go on a week's vacation with his wife Hilda. He would give his help the week off with pay and take her to visit any big city of her choice. The police suggested getting a large guard dog, something in the line of a German shepherd or a Doberman. One would think that a big man like Stash would have a large vicious dog, but that didn't fit his character. Instead of one large dog, he had two of the cutest little canines on earth.

Stash was over six feet four inches tall with very broad shoulders and the arms of a blacksmith. He always parted his thinning salt-and-pepper hair in the middle and combed it straight back. It enhanced his large Roman nose, protruding ears and a firm square jaw, which also added to his massiveness. Those who met him for the first time stood in awe at the size of him. The average height of men in those days was well under six feet. Even though Stash looked menacing, he had the disposition of a teddy bear and a heart of gold. There wasn't a mean bone in his monstrous body. The only time he used his dominance was when he asked an unruly customer to leave. Stash ran a peaceful fun-loving tavern, which made it the choice of all the neighborhood bars in town. Kiddy-corner across the street from Stash's was the northeast corner gate of the Greenwood Cemetery. There were many Saturday nights when the police would see some drunk starting to go through that gate thinking he was entering his own property. Some customers would stagger deeper into the grounds, get lost and then sleep it off on a grave until dawn. It was unfortunate that on one winter morning a customer was found slumped over a tombstone frozen to death, proving 'bath-tub gin isn't good anti-freeze.'

There was always some kind of activity going on at the bar. Stash sponsored many sporting events like a pool league, horseshoe pitching contests and Stash's own baseball team. Local men that played other neighborhood taverns in a round-robin schedule made up the team. On Friday nights, you could get a fish fry dinner for only fifty cents. There were polka dances on Saturday nights from eight until the last customer went home. Stash always booked the best Polish dance band in the area. He believed if you wanted to hear good Polish music it took an old Polish musician to play it. The leader of the band was Peter Petroski who had four sidemen, every one of them well up in their years and bald as a bowling ball. Stash advertised the band as Peter and his ...Four Skins. It took me a long time to find out what the people were laughing at when they read that sign. I did not get it until my friend, a character we called Snort, explained it to me. I am certainly glad I asked him and not my ma.

I can see by the puzzled look on your face that I haven't told you tell about Snort yet. He comes later on in the story and I am sure you will get a big kick out of him.

Chapter 11

Stash's wife Hilda stood about five foot six with long blond hair worn in a French braid. She had the typical features of the Norwegian girl, flawless skin, dazzling light blue eyes, long shapely legs and a bust line, even Dolly Parton would have envied. When she walked, she strutted like a fashion model, causing a sensual movement of the cheeks on her bubble-butt. Customers found it difficult not to stare. It was puzzling that she would pick a man with such gargantuan features, such as Stash. We never knew much about her background and evidently, Stash never knew either. From what we learned through the grapevine, was he met her through a boat owner who worked for Al Capone running illegal whiskey out of Chicago. He made his stealthy deliveries after midnight to docks along the south shore of Lake Michigan. His stops included East Chicago, Whiting, Hammond, Gary and our port. According to the rumor floating around, he introduced Hilda as his cousin from Oslo, Norway. It was not long after meeting Hilda they were married in Chicago.

The 'older guys' wondered if it were true that all girls from Scandinavia had blond hair all over. Not one of them ever got up enough nerve to ask Stash. He would have knocked them into next week. Hilda defied all the rules of dignity, a woman of that era was supposed to adhere to. She smoked in public, drank to severe intoxication, wore revealing clothes and flirted seductively with the men at the bar. They also knew how to tease her and get her dander up, especially when she had been hitting the Captain Morgan bottle.

They would kid her about not having the typical beauty mark only found on perfect beauties. She would take it for a while, then stand up, slam her drink on the table yelling, "you damn right I've got one and if you think you're gonna get me to show it to you, you've got your brains in your friggin' balls! The only guy that gets to see where it's located on my body is my husband."

I have to stop here and tell you about this old steady customer that always sat on the same stool at the end of the bar (ala-Norm in the T.V. sit-com, "Cheers.") He summed up Hilda one time by saying, "God gave her a beautiful body, beautiful hair, beautiful eyes, beautiful mouth, stuck a tongue in it and ruined the whole works."

Hilda was not too happy with her life with Stash and there were times when she, in a state of intoxicating delirium, would start mumbling about how boring it was living in a little town like this. She said she longed for the bright lights and all the exciting things to do in those bigger cities. She kept dropping hints that maybe if the right man came along, she wouldn't think twice about leaving. There were also rumors that when Stash was out of town with his baseball team, she auditioned one or two. I couldn't believe such a beautiful woman was nothing more than a 'Shoestring.'

Chapter 12

The 'older guys,' as we referred to them, were mostly high school dropouts and only a few ever made it past the twelfth grade. They never hung out with us adolescents very much, because they considered themselves men and superior. The only time they let us play sandlot baseball with them, was when they didn't have enough to make up two teams. We stood around with baited-breath waiting for a team captain to choose us. They picked me first because I was rather good for my age. There were not any organized activities, like the 'little leagues' of today. Our equipment consisted of old used baseballs and broken bats. The bats had tacks and yards of wire and electrical tape tightly wound around the handles. The baseball gloves were hand-me-downs, but many times, we played barehanded. If a guy did have a glove, he would leave it at his position when his team came up to bat. I never owned a glove, because most of the time it wasn't needed. The old baseball had taken so many whacks it lost all its firmness. There were times the ball we used was so soft, even the older guys had a heck-of-a-time hitting it out of the infield.

I know you may be thinking I am exaggerating, but let me assure you I am not. That is the way it was during those 'depression years.' Some families were so poor they couldn't rub two pennies together.

Because of the constant arguing, I don't think we ever finished nine innings. No one wanted to be an umpire, so making a decision on a close play usually was a wrestling match between the two captains. The only time a player ever won a decision was when he would threaten to go home and take his beat-up ball with him. Although they fought among themselves, they stopped anyone from starting a fight with us kids. I think it was the "honor among thieves syndrome. The only knocking around we received, occurred while we were playing the game.

One other form of baseball they always played with us was whenever one of them passed by a kid and caught him off-guard, he would reach down and take a swipe at the fly of his pants. They hadn't invented zippers yet and pants usually had four buttons. The trick was to see how many of the buttons came loose. One was only a single, two a double and so on. The hit that they were striving for was the 'grand-slammer'...all four buttons. Many kids went home with a sore peepka. I never told my ma the reason I was losing so many buttons. If she had any idea the 'older guys' were reaching for my private area, I would never have been allowed to play with them again.

After each game, we sat around listening to them talk about their favorite big league teams and the great players like Babe Ruth. We referred to those sessions as the 'pow-wow.' The subject of their conversation started out about baseball, but invariably would always end up about sex. They all professed expertise on the subject and didn't hesitate to brag about it either. I must admit that even though I knew my ma wouldn't want me to stay and listen, I couldn't walk away from hearing anything relating to sex. I sat there completely absorbing the information and there wasn't a question about sex they didn't have an answer for. Little did we know that someday schools would hold classes on sex. They may have had some knowledge on sex, but I was the guru when we talked about major league baseball.

That was my dream and I followed the careers of some of the famous stars. There were many pow-wows that the guys sought to stump me with questions like, what were the years Babe Ruth played for the Yankees? I would immediately name them, from 1920 to 1934. Sometimes they asked, who were the Hall of Fame managers for the Yankees and I quickly informed them, Miller Huggins, 1918-1929. Those were the true statistics, but I could have made them up. They never questioned my knowledge, but sat there in complete awe. I also had a collection of baseball cards; each card had an action picture of a famous player. To get a picture card, you had to buy a pack of Bazooka bubble gum. It was a tremendous success for the gum company, because it started kids all over the United States collecting pictures of their heroic idols.

I worked feverishly at my hobby and ended up with enough baseball cards to build, not just a house of cards, but also the Empire State Building. If I had known how much they would be worth today, I could buy the Empire State Building. That is also true with saving comic books, featuring; Flash Gordon, Batman and Spiderman. I could name many more. I guess I was never the visionary-type …Oh well, such is life as they say.

Going home alone at times was dangerous for a kid. There were bullies that hid behind trees or hedges waiting to jump out and grab the unsuspecting kid in a half nelson. While in their grasp, they performed a number of tortuous acts, one of which they called a 'Knuckle-Rub'. Making a fist with the knuckle of the middle finger protruding out formed the knuckle. He then rubbed that knuckle back and forth very hard on his victims scalp. The pain was even worse if the kid had a summer crew cut. When the bully was finally satisfied, he would end the ordeal with..."Ho- ho-ho, "Look how mama's boy is crying."

Then there were those 'Monkey-Bumps'. That is when the bully used the same knuckle to rap the top of the forearm. It would cause a bump to rise and then quickly go back down. The bully got a big laugh watching the bumps, but it was no laughing matter for the kid who carried bruises for weeks.

Besides the Knuckle-Rub and Monkey-Bumps, there was still another torture. They called it...Snakebite. They grabbed the kid's arm with both hands and while squeezing hard gave a twist in opposite directions. What that had to do with a snakebite I don't know. I guess the twisting of the hands resemble the movement of the snake's head while inserting his poisonous fangs.

I thought at the time the tortuous bully acts would end some day, but the pain and embarrassment is even more rampant today. They never picked on the kids with older and bigger brothers. I didn't have a brother, but did not need one. I had a friend named Snort. I know I still haven't told you about Snort, but be patient.

Chapter 13

Greenwood Cemetery was more than just a burial site. It was a fascinating place to learn about the history of our city. The dates on the tombstones revealed the change in life spans, the settling of our city and the occurrence of many epidemics. Names indicated the ethnic backgrounds as well as the inter-marriages between a few families in our small community. Birthplaces and military duties were also included in some inscriptions. If you saw the letters G.A.R. (GRAND ARMY OF THE REPUBLIC), it meant that the deceased fought for the North in the Civil War. Greenwood was at one time part of the farm our house stood on. It was a hilly site, difficult for farming, but perfect for cemetery viewing.

From a mesa-like-top in the middle, it gradually sloped down on all sides to a wrought-iron fence that surrounded it. Four streets bordered the shape of Greenwood Cemetery. There was Barker Avenue on the north and Greenwood Avenue on the South. The east and west streets were Jackson on the east and Tilden on the west. All four corners of the cemetery had a gate. Halfway between each corner-gate was a smaller gate, which was right across the street from our house. The main entrance was on Tilden Street, halfway between the corner of Greenwood and Barker Avenue. It was the most impressive of all the entrances. Beautiful green yews flanked the majestic high arched ivy-covered wall. Fifteen-foot wrought-iron gates swung out in opposite directions to welcome the hearse and funeral processions. Greenwood Cemetery was a perfect name for it.

A variety of beautifully manicured pines lined both sides of the service roads that stayed green throughout the four seasons. The sight of white snow clinging on green branches after a snowstorm caused many artists to run for their brushes.

My ma could name all thirty-five different varieties of fir trees and their origination. She described each cone the tree produced. Her favorite one was the Arborvitae. It made a tea rich in vitamin C and was extremely beneficial to health. She called it the 'tree of life.'

I used to look forward to the walks we took on Sundays. My ma cut baskets of flowers from her garden and used them to dress up the neglected graves. She said it was a shame that people forgot loved ones so soon. She never left without kneeling and saying a prayer for the person whose name was on the headstone. As we passed the graves, I couldn't help thinking about all the dark secrets laid to rest in those caskets six feet below. It would give a professional writer an endless amount of material for a biography.

The pump-house was directly across the street from the main gate on Tilden. The city remodeled an old house and used the front room for the cemetery's business office. The crew-foreman used the back bedroom, kitchen and bath. They called it the pump-house because of the large black lift pump out in front. It had a long curved handle and the depth of the well was five hundred feet. Most people needed to use both hands to start bringing the water up. They came from all over the city to fill their large canteens with that crystal cool uncontaminated water. The property behind the building boarded the workhorse. She was the typical old gray mare that pulled a flatbed trailer with wheels that looked like they came off one of the original covered wagons. You couldn't tell who was older, the wagon or the horse, they both sagged in the middle. It would be a few years before the pump-house had a motorized tractor and for that old nag I am sure, its arrival couldn't come any too soon.

The foreman of the cemetery's work crew was Daniel P. Dugan. I think the P stood for Patrick. He fit the description of what many thought of the Irish back then...hard workers and heavy drinkers. You had only to look at him to see the telltale signs of one who spent many years of abuse on an alcoholic diet. His blood-shot eyes looked like they were about to pop out at any moment. If they had blood banks back then, he could have gone down and had his eyes drained. Along with that, he had the drinker's nose with its bluish-hue at the tip. He also had the flushed reddish face with areas of little broken capillaries. I don't think Dugan ever knew how high his blood pressure was. Back then, blood pressure wasn't a health problem. Dugan wore his hair in a crew-cut style and always wore the favorite cap he designed and created himself. He fashioned it from an old felt hat by removing the brim and folding the bottom material up around the base. He completely adorned the hat with an array of button pins. There were campaign buttons, company logos and names of girls. Even some of his favorite baits for fly-fishing were hooked on. He was very proud of his millinery achievement, but it looked out of place on the head of a fifty-year-old man. In those days it was called a beanie and popular with grade school kids. Dugan got the nickname 'Dig-it Dugan' because he had trouble understanding the layout diagram of the cemetery posted up on the office wall. They laid the grave lots out systematically and numbered. For example, the order sheet could read north division one-block three-lot two-grave number seven. The more he nipped the more confused he got. There were times old Dig-it Dugan and his crew would start digging at a site and discover they were working in the wrong area. He would then leave that project and go looking for the correct location and fill the half-dug grave later. Sometimes it took weeks before his crew came back to fill up those holes. There was a saying that old Dig-it Dugan left more unearthed ground than all the cemetery animals put together. The 'older guys' were always teasing him by asking, "where in the hell ya gonna dig it today Dugan?"

The property behind the pump-house had a small barn and several sheds used for the many tools needed to run an efficient cemetery. The barn had a stall for the mare where they stored her hay and oats.

He called his workhorse the 'Bitch'. She was nicknamed that by the 'older guys,' who would hear Dig-it out in the cemetery berating the horse for not moving at his commands. People  blocks away could hear his tenor voice yelling, "Move it you old Bitch." It was 'old Bitch' this and 'old Bitch' that, thus the moniker, 'old Bitch.' It may have sounded like Dig-it Dugan hated the tired old nag, but he was never known to whip the horse or hurt her in any way. He would not allow any one of his crew to lay a hand on her either. If one ever did, that little five-foot-two Irishman would be all over him in a minute. It was also a known fact that you had better not mess with an Irishman when he gets mad, even if he is only five-foot- two.

At the end of each day's work Dig-it Dugan unhooked the trailer, took off the Bitch's harness and pushed her head first into a stall so narrow her flanks rubbed against the sides. The trough that held the feed for the horse was in back of the stall. When she finished eating, he had to back her out, turn her around and shove her back in again. The only thing that held her in was a two by four strung across the front. I think the need of a two by four was superfluous. By the end of the day's work, the old nag was so tired; she didn't have enough energy to bat the flies away with her tail.

On Friday nights while the old Bitch and flies were dining, Dig-it Dugan couldn't wait to go north three blocks on Tilden to Stash's tavern. He would sit on his favorite barstool, drinking Irish whiskey until closing time. Week after week Dig-it Dugan staggered back to the pump-house, invariable tripping over the same raised portions of a sidewalk and ended up flopping down on a pile of hay next to the Bitch's stall. He would stay there passed out until noon on Saturday and when he awoke, wondered how he skinned his knees.

I don't want you to get the wrong impression about the 'older guys.' They were rather crude when it came to moral values, but cared deeply about the suffering of others, especially animals. Back then; as it is today, some pet owners caused animals to suffer when going on trips by neglecting to see that Fido or Tabby had plenty of food and water. Dig-it Dugan probably didn't realize the hardship the 'old Bitch' was experiencing the nights he spent at Stash's tavern. I don't think he ever considered her a pet, but another fellow worker. Many times after the long day's labor, he left her standing for hours in that narrow stall. She was unable to lie down, or move in any direction. Then on top of that, there were those sweltering hot summer nights. I don't think Dig-it realized what the 'old Bitch' was going through. I'm sure a lot of the pet owners do not place themselves into what the animals must endure.

The 'older guys' realizing what the animal went through on Dig-it's inebriation nights, would take turns seeing that the old horse didn't suffer. The guys knew his Friday night habit and waited behind the office until he was snoring away. Then very quickly removed the two by four and led the workhorse out of the stall to the mounds of hay in the manger, where she would lay down to recuperate After replacing the two by four across the stalls entrance, they would give each other high-fives and proudly disappear into the night.

To see the mare lounging in the hay on Saturday mornings drove Dig-it out of his mind. He just couldn't believe a dumb horse would know how to remove the two by four. He spent many hours Friday nights at the tavern, bragging about the smart horse he had. It also drove him to the height of frustration trying to get the patrons of Stash's tavern to believe his claims. Most of them saw Dig-it as a flaky old-in-the-tooth alcoholic anyway. Some even said they could see the horse using her head to lift the barrier up and out, but how did the animal put it back up, or even bother to.

When the 'older guys' heard all the fuss being made of their concern for the 'old Bitch,' they swore to keep it a secret among themselves and ordered us kids to do the same.

Chapter 14

My favorite summertime fun was skinny-dipping. The swimming hole was located on the outskirts of town, formed by a sharp bend in Trail Creek as it flowed on its way to become the mouth of the city's famous harbor. The area was so dense with trees and bushes that I wondered how any one discovered it. Swimming in the nude had nothing to do with sex. We were just a bunch of naked boys having fun in our own Garden of Eden and we never bothered wearing fig leaves either. We tried to keep the place a secret so the girls wouldn't find it. If they ever started coming out there, we would have to wear our darn bathing suits. At that age, we weren't interested in girls anyway. We felt superior to them because we had a peepka between our legs and they didn't. We were going to be a man and a girl...only a woman. We considered it a man's world back then because only three years before my birth, women couldn't even vote. Before the civil war, a woman couldn't hold any office in the United States either. Even in the Bible scriptures according to St. Paul stated, "That women keep silent and be in subjection." It took thirty years of enactment of laws to allow women to control their own earnings or have equal guardianship of children after a divorce. Along with that, you can include control and property ownership to share in a deceased husband's estate, or enter into any occupation or profession.

I wonder how my ma could have ever survived under those conditions if they hadn't changed. She told me many times, if it weren't for a woman named Susan B. Anthony, women would still be living in conditions of the seventeenth century. In 1919, Congress finally passed the Susan B. Anthony Suffrage Amendment, the right of all citizens to vote, male or female. My ma was a staunch Democrat and worked her spare time as a precinct committee member. She even got the city to rent our house for a voting place. She never missed the chance to make an extra buck. It took a lot of effort to move the furniture into the bedrooms and even some chairs into that damp cellar. Her biggest worry was if Diabel liked chewing on varnish. Even though women were on par with men, we still weren't ready to give up our supremacy, because of our plumbing between our legs.

I don't think our secret swimming place was a secret from the girls, because there were times we swore we heard giggling coming from behind the large bushes that lined the riverbank.

The 'older guys' never bothered coming out to swim with us. They preferred the challenge of the deep waters of Lake Michigan. Some of them were so athletic they could make it out to the milepost, rest on the buoy and then swim back. Others risked their lives diving off the lighthouse in-between narrow gaps of large cement boulders that surrounded its base. When they wanted to swim nude, there was a hush-hush adult area called West Beach. It was on the other side of the town's most famous sand dune, 'The Hoosier Slide.'

I still believe that to this day God created the swimming hole just for us. It had the typical oak tree with a large limb conveniently hanging over the water. It made an ideal place to hang a tire swing. There was always a line of kids waiting to swing out, holding their noses yelling 'canon-ball' and landing ass first in the water, which made a loud smacking sound. It was a funny sight to see the red dupa's running up the bank for another turn.

Although the kids came from a lot of different neighborhoods and nationalities, there weren't any racial arguments. We were just kids having fun in our own wonderful Utopia. Along with the game of tag, dive for the penny, or who could swing out over the water the farthest. We did one routine just for laughs. A kid would float on his back exposing his peepka and yell out... pickle on a plate...pickle on a plate. If he was German, it would Bratwurst... pickle on a plate and Polish, a Kielbasa... pickle on a plate and so on. The biggest laugh came when the Jewish kid yelled, Kosher pickle on a plate... with Matzo balls.

Going home was a big letdown for me. I felt like I was leaving heaven and going back to the hell my stepfather Frank would be raising. Many times I found him standing over my ma drunk to the gills shouting about the dumb move he made by getting married. Through all his ranting and raving she would keep right on preparing his favorite supper and dessert.

I must confess there were times I had to stifle my thought. My ma said wishing bad things for someone was a terrible thing to do.

Speaking of nude beaches, why is it, most nudists are people you don't want to see naked.

Chapter 15

Henry 'Snort' Erickson was a high school senior, but never had anything to do with the 'older guys.' His features gave the impression of being somewhat of a hayseed, making him the sucker of most of their pranks. Snort was a good-natured kid and took their teasing in stride. He was captain of the wrestling team and if he ever lost his temper, he could have wiped out the whole bunch. He had the facial features to become a great comic. His straw-blond hair looked like each strand had a mind of its own and his slightly bucked teeth under a long thin freckled nose, reminded me of Mortimer Snerd. That was the dummy used by a famous ventriloquist, Edgar Bergen. Snort was far from being a dummy and carried a B+ average all through high school.

They gave him the nickname 'Snort' because of the way he laughed. He had the strangest way of breathing air back through his nostrils that made a snorting sound. Snort liked to tell jokes and when he delivered the punch line, he would slap his knee and start laughing...ha-ha-ha-snort...ha-ha-ha...snort. It didn't take long until we were all rolling on the ground holding our sides with uncontrollable laughter. It wasn't at Snort's joke but at Snort's snorting. He didn't realize he made that sound and thought it was his joke that made us laugh so hard.

He was like an older brother to me and was always there when I needed him. I would go to him for answers that had anything to do about sex, not my ma or the 'older guys.' Snort was the only boy in a family of four kids, so my lack of knowledge about girls' private parts led me to ask him, "Snort, have you seen any of your sisters without their clothes on?"

He didn't hesitate to say, "Hell, Michael, when we were younger we all took baths together on Saturdays."

"Then how are they different from boys?

"Michael, girls don't have a pickle between their legs." Whenever he thought he said something funny, he would quickly ride off on his bike laughing and snorting. He never gave me a chance for further questions, like, "What do they have there, Snort?" His information was, "Girls conveniently had a hole there." When I heard that, I immediately wondered how they kept water from going up into their belly.

As I tell it now, I can't believe how naïve I was.

Knowing I could trust Snort with anything I held private, I told him about how I placed my peepka between my thighs and asked him if he ever did that.

"Jeez Michael, if you are getting that urge, just take it out and whack it." Then he pedaled off again laughing and snorting, leaving me wondering why I would ever want to give it a whack... I wasn't mad at it.

Chapter 16

After grandfather passed away, Frank's disposition changed dramatically. His commitment to be a husband and father was obliviously one he never really wanted. In fact, his drinking kept getting worse and he was staying away from the house for longer periods. There were weeks on end that he never came home. Although my ma had a husband, she and I were virtually living alone.

It was after a baseball game that I heard some disturbing news. An 'older guy' at the pow-wow said a rumor was spreading that some of the crew was using the tugboats for shacking-up. I couldn't believe Frank was cheating on a wonderful person like my ma, but then again, he wasn't coming home. She asked where he had been sleeping and he told her out on the boat. He said the tug had a bunk bed, kitchen and toilet. He went on to explain that the fish were in such abundance; the nets were filling up beyond capacity. All I feel like doing after the long hours is hitting the sack early.

When my ma told me Frank's excuse, I wanted to tell her the gossip the 'older guys' were spreading. I remembered her saying, "Never accuse anyone of anything unless it was absolutely true." That would bear false witness against thy neighbor. I really didn't know for sure if Frank was one of those sailors doing the shacking-up, so I kept the rumor to myself. I don't think my Aunt Helen, who never trusted Frank in the first place, ever believed his lame excuse. When Frank did show up, he brought his duffel bag jammed with clothing reeking from the smell of fish. I often wondered what the people on the bus thought about the stench emanating from the bulging bag. It is a wonder they didn't throw it out the window and Frank along with it.

For some reason he never had a driver's license or drove a car. He used the bus when he was going straight home, but for bar hopping on Friday nights, he hired a cab for the evening. On those nights, Frank would end up blowing his whole paycheck. It was frustrating for my ma who took the same vows he did and worked very hard to keep a roof over our heads. As far as I was concerned, I was glad he stayed away. When he did come home, he was always drunk and very abusive towards her. I feared that someday he would hurt her badly. There were times when I noticed bruises on her face and arms and asked her how she got them. She would say, "Don't worry, Januscheck, they soon will go away."

There was one time when Frank came home yelling and screaming, that I heard what sounded like furniture thrown around. I quickly ran down the stairs from my bedroom and what I saw made me want to break the commandment, *thou shalt not kill*. With the help of a kitchen chair, my ma was struggling to rise up from the floor. I knew then that he must have hit her. I started after him, but at my age what could I possibly do. I deemed it wiser to go back to see if she needed any help.

I told Aunt Helen what Frank was doing and asked her to try to talk my ma into divorcing him. She said, "I'll try Michael, but she knows what the church law is on divorcing. Your mother would never go against the church and firmly believes in the vows, 'for better or for worse' and until 'death do us part.' I am sure she doesn't want the title, 'divorcee.' It's a stigma of shame given to a woman a husband didn't want anymore."

The only answer to my ma's problem I thought would be the last statement in the marriage vow... 'Till death do us part.' I knew I couldn't commit that crime and for that matter, none of us could. I was hoping somebody else would do it; like a jealous boyfriend or maybe an angry husband, who found Frank messing with his wife. While working at Stash's bar, Aunt Helen heard that many guys hated his flirtatious behavior around their women.

It wasn't long after I made that wish that it almost came true. My ma awoke to a telephone call at three in the morning. It was the police informing her Frank was in the hospital and immediately told her not to worry, it wasn't anything life threatening. They asked her to come down and sign for his release.

As time went on, I learned piece by piece what happened to Frank. A police officer making his tour around the cemetery spotted Frank's body slumped against the fence. At first, the cop thought it was just another inebriated customer who passed out on his way home from Stash's tavern. When he stood Frank up, he saw it wasn't too much whiskey that caused his condition. Frank's face had blood around the nose, lips and his right eye swollen almost closed. He said when he stood Frank up, his pants fell down around the ankles. While pulling them back up, he noticed a large smear of blood on the crotch area of the underwear. He said it looked like an emergency and immediately rushed him to the hospital.

At that time of the morning, the emergency crew was usually under-staffed. This particular morning it was even worse. The regular doctor had taken ill and a young intern was covering for him. When they got Frank up on the operating table, they discovered where the bleeding was coming from. The tip of Frank's penis was missing. The intern made a quick suture of the wound and stopped the bleeding. They got Frank's name and telephone number from his wallet and called my ma. What she did about the incident or whether she even questioned Frank, I never heard. I asked Aunt Helen if my ma had told her anything about it. "Michael, I don't think your mother really cares anymore."

The next day the same police officer stopped at our house and handed me a piece of paper to give to her. He said it was a note they found pinned to Frank's underwear. Evidently, it was a message from the perpetrator of the crime.

It took several weeks for his wound to heal and the stitches removed. From then on every time Frank took a leak, he would come out of the bathroom swearing to high heaven about the lousy job the young intern did on his dick. It seemed he never knew which direction the pee was going to take. Consequently, it made more work for my ma. She had to follow him in and wash those yellow streaks that ran down the white bathroom walls. I later learned that there was more to the beating incident. When my ma read the note from the officer, she laid it on the dining room table. I felt that as long as she left it out in plain view like that, it wasn't very personal, so curiosity killed the cat and I read the message to Frank written in bold letters: ***This time the tip - keep it in your pants or the next time <u>ALL</u> of it.*** The word **ALL** was underlined.

I couldn't get the image of a guy standing naked without a hose hanging down between his legs. How would he pee? Then again, what would I have to stuff between my thighs while watching the Saturday night orgies? I never dreamed that someday there would be humans changing their sexes, by legally approved operations. I also wondered if the sailor, Frank Dramski had his dick cut off... would he be considered a "Wave?" In case you didn't get it, that's what they called female sailors during World War II.

Chapter 17

As I grew older, my ma allowed me to stay out later at night, especially during summer vacation. We played a game after dark called 'Ditch.' It was a form of 'hide and seek,' but we liked our name better, because it didn't sound as childish. The participants were kids from our immediate neighborhood and all of them same age, give or take a few months. Ten kids made it just right, because the rules were that we team up in pairs. One pair would be the seekers, while the four other pairs would run off to hide. We took turns at being the seekers and set an alarm clock for a half an hour. If the seekers hadn't found you in that amount of time, the alarm would go off and you would be... 'home free.' If they did find the hiding place, they would yell... *CAPTURED!*

The possibilities for hiding places could be under steps, up in a tree, behind some stacks of lumber, under a pile of raked fall leaves or whatever other clever idea you could dream up. The only stipulation was you couldn't hide in someone's house. There wasn't any rule however, about the cemetery. I think when the rules were made; they didn't believe anyone was brave enough to go in among the tombstones, especially in the pitch-darkness of night. I had no fear of the eerie surroundings and used it one time when Mildred asked me if she could be my partner. I held the boastful distinction of never being caught. I guess Mildred and her other partners always were.

Mildred Hanklin lived directly across from us on Cloud Street. She was the only girl in our neighborhood who played 'Ditch.' Although she was our age, you could see that she was maturing a little faster than we were. The grown-ups believed she was somewhat of a tomboy. At that time maybe she was, but with her strawberry-blond hair that hung in waves down to the small of her back and enchanting transparent green eyes, she was well on her way to becoming a very beautiful Fraulein. I was always quite in awe of her and was excited that she asked me to be her partner.

Leaning against a tree with their arms blinding their eyes, the seekers started counting up to one hundred. I took Mildred by the hand and headed across Barker Avenue toward the cemetery gate. When she saw where we were headed, she became reluctant and I am sure, sorry she had me for a partner. She started to protest at first, but I gave her the keep quiet finger up to my mouth and led her to the gate. I got the idea to hide in the cemetery at breakfast that morning and greased the hinges so they wouldn't squeak.

I could hear the seekers nearing a hundred in their count and fearing they would see us, I pulled forcibly on her arm. When she felt the urgency in my action, she allowed me to lead us through the gate, into the cemetery. In our haste, we stumbled over a mound of dirt and fell into a small ditch. The seekers heard the noise we made and they quickly ran up to the fence with their flashlights and started scanning the area. Evidently, they were afraid to venture any further and just stood outside the fence.

It took a little while to realize that Mildred and I had fallen into one of old Dig-its partially dug graves. While the beam of the flashlights crossed back and forth over our heads, we laid there with her back pressing against me. As we were maneuvering our bodies to get as low as possible, I told Mildred to hold still. I was never that close to a girl before and became overwhelmed by the scent of intoxicating perfume. I never knew Mildred wore perfume. With that aroma going up my nostrils and her soft body pressing against mine, that terrible aching started in my groin. I whispered in her ear, "Please stop squirming." When I couldn't stand it any longer, I reached down and pushed my peepka between my thighs. While the seekers stood outside the fence, we hid in that pit...her squirming and me squeezing. It didn't take long until I had one of the strongest contractions ever.

While we waited for the alarm to sound, I wondered if Mildred knew why I had been breathing so hard. She must have gotten over her fear of the cemetery, because she too seemed a lot calmer.

Hearing the call... *HOME FREEEEE*, we approached the starting point far down the line from where we had been hiding. In that way, no one could see us coming out of the cemetery. When we climbed back over the fence, I noticed that I had twisted my right ankle stumbling into that ditch. It was strange I didn't feel the hurt lying next to Mildred. When I told my ma how it happened, she got out the Epson salts and hot water. That was her treatment for any sprain. Lying in bed, I wondered how Dig-it Dugan could make such a blunder digging in that undeveloped area. I was also feeling ashamed of myself for what I had done, but what the heck; I did not touch my peepka or touch Mildred with it. I also wondered if Mildred knew what happened in our secret hiding place.

I remember what one of the 'older guys' told us on that subject. He said some girls allow a guy to get in between their legs, but only if he kept his dick in his pants. Back then, they called it a 'dry hump.' Today they have another name for it, 'SAFE SEX.

Before I fell asleep that night, I wondered if they considered what I did with Mildred in that ditch, a 'dry hump.' I am sure she wouldn't let me do anything like that, because her father, you see... was a preacher; but then again, why the perfume?

Chapter 18

While working at the tavern Aunt Helen talked Stash into hiring me to bus dishes Friday nights. He must have liked my work because he kept finding other things for me to do around the tavern. The one job I always looked forward to was babysitting his two little dogs, Snowflake and Curly. He acquired them from customers who hoped he would accept a pup to help defer their delinquent bar bills. Stash being a soft touch, accepted. He went along with his end of the bargain, but had to stop any more trade-offs by saying, "I can't buy supplies with animals." The customers kept their word and before long each one brought a cute little puppy with papers from the A.K.C.

As it turned out, Stash got the runt of the each litter. I am sure he could have called the deal off, but once he held them, he kept them. The longer Stash had the pups the deeper his love grew. If he ever thought of giving the dogs away someday, he made a big mistake by naming them. My ma warned me, if you give it a name, it then becomes your pet.

Snowflake and Curly would never have made good watchdogs. Being so friendly, they would rather run up and lick the face of any intruder, than scare him away. I don't think they even knew how to growl, let alone bark. The dogs made whimpering sounds of happiness whenever people stopped to pet them... and no one could ever resist that urge. I told Stash many times if he couldn't keep them at the tavern, I would take them off his hands. He would say, "Michael, I would give up the bar first."

Snowflake was a little female from the White Terrier breed, which is the smallest of the terrier strain. She had eyes that hid under shaggy eyebrows and a little black pug nose that twitched whenever she wagged her tail, which was constantly. The A.K.C. report on White Terriers was that they are alert, courageous, and very friendly and loved to romp and play in the snow. I found the description hit the nail right on the head, for Snowflake.

Curly was an American Cocker Spaniel, the smallest breed of Spaniel. His beautiful brown and white shiny fur lay in waves along the length of his body. He was of the 'puppy-mill variety;' gentle and very playful. Stash had papers on the dogs, but never gave any thought on using them for breeding purposes. He said he only wanted them for pets. I had the silly mental picture of Curly trying to mount a bitch in heat and have trouble getting high enough to insert his little pickle.

Stash's pets never grew anywhere near what they considered runt-size and looked like little animated stuffed toys. They were very happy animals and constantly at play. Whenever I needed to stop for a moments rest, they would start chasing each other around until I was ready to go again. There were five tricks apiece that Stash had taught them and each dog had his own routine. They were such little hams, that at the sound of the word 'trick,' they would immediately go through all five without stopping. It was quite hilarious to watch Curly walking on his back legs or sitting up begging; at the same time that Snowflake was doing her back flips and rollovers. You would think you were watching a three-ring circus. What was also amazing was the fact they never expected any treat for their performances.

Whenever Stash and Hilda went on a vacation, I got the fun job of watching Snowflake and Curly. Walking the two blocks to my house, the dogs would get so excited their pull on the leash made me run to keep up with them. It didn't take many doggy-sitting times until they realized that every time they saw Stash loading suitcases in his car, it was another trip to my house. The dogs knew the routine so well, they didn't wait for the leashes, but made the trip on their own. They were very obedient animals. No matter how excited they were at play, when you said stop, they immediately ceased their activities. Snowflake and Curly won the hearts of everyone they met.

My ma of course adored them and I am sure Aunt Helen, and Uncle Steve felt the same way. I didn't think Dupa had anything but hatred for the dogs. It was obvious he didn't like it when Frank petted them, or never flipped them in the air with his foot. In all the time I knew Frank, petting the little dogs was the only bit of affection he showed to anything and you could see how jealous Dupa was. Snowflake and Curly were well aware of Dupa's hatred for them and always sensed when he was around. There were many times they suddenly stopped playing and stared in the same direction. When I looked in the area they were staring at, I would spot Dupa peering from behind some bush or up in a tree. I think Snowflake and Curly knew cats didn't like dogs, no matter how cute they are.

I must tell you how fortunate I was to have found the true meaning of unconditional love so early in my life. It came from my mother and two little canines named, Snowflake and Curly.

Chapter 19

The southern shores of Lake Michigan are renowned for beaches and towering sand dunes. Through the years, strong northerly winds blowing off the lake created them. It lifted grains of sand and transported them inland, where plants and hills slowed the wind causing it to drop its sandy cargo. On windy days, I could build my own little sand dune by placing my shoe on a blanket and watch the sand slowly forming on its opposite side. If I didn't disturb it until I went home, there would be a little sand hill as high as the shoe itself. This process today is more apparent on Mt. Baldy, which they called a 'live dune'. The beach grasses and cottonwood trees can't hold nature's dynamic forces and you can see Baldy slowly change year by year.

In my teens, I spent many days of my summer vacations on our beautiful beach. My first visit though, was at night when I was just a little boy. The city had been sweltering for weeks in one of our typical dog-day summers. The relief of an air conditioner wasn't in existence back then and any fan would just blow more hot air, making matters even worse. After suffering through one restless night, my ma said, "let us go sleep on the beach, Januscheck."

"But ma isn't the beach closed at night?"

"Yes, but they have opened it up for the public during the hot spell."

You could always count on cool breezes coming off Lake Michigan and this night was no exception. We could feel the change in the temperature as soon as we stepped out of the car. Holding my hand, my ma led me through the hundreds of cars in the dark parking lot. The city was allowing people on the beach, but didn't turn on the lights to save on the city's electric bill. The lack of moonlight made it difficult to see where we were heading. There were so many people on the beach that my ma had difficulty leading us through the maze of bodies snuggled under blankets. The snoring was so loud, it sounded like a farmer just fed a new supply of slop to his hogs. My ma finally found a space to spread out our blanket. I learned that the early arrivals would lie down at water's edge, where cool waves lapped against their bare feet. I couldn't understand how anyone could fall sleep that way, especially if the water ever reached as high as their peepka. The atmospheric conditions were hard to believe. People in town were desperately trying to keep cool, while just a few blocks north they were under blankets. My ma, who had been working all day in the heat, immediately fell asleep. If it wasn't for some woman moaning under a blanket next to us, I too could have gone to sleep. She kept it up until I felt so concerned about her I woke up my ma.

"Why did you wake me, Januscheck, what's the matter?"

"I think there is something wrong with that lady over there."

She turned and whispered, "She probably has stomach cramps from heat sickness. She will feel better in a little while, just go to sleep."

I finally did, but only after I could hear the lady was feeling much better. It seemed the cramps didn't last too long and the moaning was now replaced with giggling sounds. (Well, I told you I was just a little boy.)

There were many days spent on that beautiful beach, but most of my nights were with my neighborhood pals. We were constantly coming up with some creative activity, right up until the time we had to go in. One of the many things we did besides playing Ditch was something we called ...Kill a bat, which I was all for. I was just about to fall asleep one night, when I heard a fluttering of what sounded like a bird. A bat had flown on my bedroom curtain. When I told the family what I had discovered, we went on a safari with brooms, fly swatters and rolled-up newspapers, looking for its hiding place. We even opened the windows in hopes it would want to escape back to its habitat. It never would leave and it made periodic trips, flying from one bedroom to the other. I bet I was the only boy growing up with a killer rat in the basement, a vampire bat upstairs, and a house situated across the street from a spooky old cemetery. Rats and bats aren't exactly household pets.

Now back to "Kill a bat". We tied a white cloth on the end of an eighteen-foot bamboo-fishing pole, stood under the corner streetlight and waved the cloth back and forth. As soon as the bat's radar caught the fluttering sound of that cloth, it made a swooping attack thinking it was a winged insect drawn to the glow of the light. When the bat hit the cloth, it went down where we immediately beat it to death with baseball bats. (Again, no pun intended.)

We thought they were rabid lice-infected rodents with wings that got so tangled up in women's hair; the only way to extract them was to cut them loose with scissors. Even movies showed how terrible bats were. There was this heinous vampire called Dracula, played by Bela Lagosi, who needed to drink blood to survive. He slept all day in a casket, and then at night he would come out, turn himself into a vampire bat and proceeded to suck women dry. Being a male didn't relieve any of my fears ... blood is blood. Therefore, we thought, 'kill a bat' was helping our environment by getting rid of them. How wrong we were. As I look back on it now, I bare a terrible regret for participating. The only easing of my conscious is realizing that at the time, we didn't know the truth about bats.

There were other times we just sat around on my front porch telling ghost stories. The kids seemed to like my stories the best. They couldn't get enough of my creativity and were always begging me to make up a real thriller. I was amazed at my ability to start the story without knowing just where I was going and somehow make it up as I went along. I can still picture the excited expressions on their young faces as they anxiously awaited those scary endings. I don't think I ever disappointed them and I always got a round of applause for my effort. It was fun telling those stories and I never passed up a request to tell one. Some were so good I almost believed them myself.

There was one time however; they didn't want to hear my creative effort. It was when I informed them I was going to tell my next ghost story in the dark of night, over in the cemetery among the tombstones. I razzed them by saying they were all 'scaredy cats.' My ma once told me that God gives us all a special gift. Uncle Steve's gift was a terrific mind for figures and looking back on it now, I think God must have wanted me to be a writer.

Speaking of ghosts, one of the eeriest things I ever saw took place on a bright moonlit summer night. I awoke around three in the morning by a haunting sound coming from the cemetery. I knew there weren't any wolves in our area, but the 'who-o-o-o' sure sounded like one. I trembled at the thought that maybe I was about to see what everyone feared was out there... a ghost. I got the telescope and headed for my bedroom window. The howling was echoing through the trees and resounding off tombstones, sending a series of chilling shivers up and down my spine. It was hard to determine the exact spot the weird sound was coming from. I was about to give up when my lens caught the sight of a white object. I realized it wasn't a ghost at all, but a large white dog standing on a freshly flower-covered grave and howling up at the moon. The dog must have been a family pet of the deceased. It was a complete mystery to me how the dog ever found the exact burial site. Back then; there wasn't any knowledge about cadaver dogs.

My playmates were so innocently naïve, they were gullible for any kind of story. One time I told them about my grandfather feeding the squirrels. I informed them how we loaded him down with shelled peanuts and wheeled him out into the front yard. I related to them how I stood hidden on the porch and watched the squirrels coming from the cemetery across the street. I told them how funny it was to see them frantically climbing over one another to get to those tasty peanuts and they must have numbered in the hundreds. I went on to tell them, how at the height of their frantic search for the goodies, the squirrels' completely obliterated grandfather, who nodded back to sleep as soon as they left. With 'tongue-in-cheek,' I told them that one time when I was about to replace grandfather's hat, a large bushy-tailed squirrel came cautiously down the trunk of one of our elm trees that fronted our property. I was curious to see what the squirrel was up to and I thought he was coming back to make sure there wasn't just one more peanut to be found. I continued on how I watched him drop down to the sidewalk, run over to grandfather's hat and pick it up. While carrying the hat in his mouth, the squirrel scampered up grandfather's sleeve, onto his shoulder, stood up and placed it back on his head. Within seconds, the squirrel was up the tree and out of sight. I couldn't believe that for weeks on end, kids would point out a squirrel and ask, "Is that the one you saw Michael?"

I was always fooling and teasing them whenever I could. I even had them believing I was an expert piano player. We had a player piano in our living room and at least a hundred rolls of popular songs of the 20's and 30's. My trick was to insert a roll and shut the two sliding doors that hid the compartment. While playing on our porch, I would interrupt whatever we were doing and tell them I would be right back because I had to practice my piano. They stayed on the porch with their noses pressing against our living room window, looking in to watch and listen to me play. With the sofa blocking the view of my feet pumping the bellows and my hands moving up and down the keys, I pretended I was actually playing. I believe that to this day they never caught on.

My amazing mother was the one who could really play the piano. I sat next to her and sang lead while she added the harmony. We made a great team my ma and me. Everything she did was prize-winning caliber. Like the time she entered us in a contest at the Indiana Days parade, which took place on July 4, the last day of a three-day celebration. The rules were those with the best costume and portrayals would win a fifty-mile boat ride on the luxurious three-deck passenger liner, the Theodore Roosevelt. When my ma told me what the first prize was, I couldn't wait for the day of the parade. I knew she had a great sense of humor and with her creative ability; she could come up with a super idea for our costumes.

She had me dressed to look like Huckleberry Finn with faded bib overalls and a checkered red flannel shirt. She cut the pant legs short with jagged edges. The only other accessories were a beat-up plantation straw hat and a tree branch with a red bandana tied at one end. She said it would really look authentic if at times I would skip along whistling a happy tune.

My ma dressed like the famous mime-actor, Charlie Chaplin. She wore a black suit with a tight-fitting coat and baggy pants. The white shirt had a high starched collar and a black string tie. She also painted a black Hitler-style mustache under her nose and arched her eyebrows. Add to that, shoes with spats, a cane and a black derby. She not only looked like Charlie Chaplin, but she had every one of his movements down pat, with her quick short little steps, the waddle in her walk and twirling of a walking cane. I didn't know how my ma could do it, but at intervals, she would stop, jump up sideways and click her heels, as Chaplin did. You can add the twitching of her little mustache and rapid up and down movement of the heavy painted eyebrows.

Indiana Days had different themes and activities for each of the three days. Sometimes July can get as hot as any day in August and this year was no exception. For two weeks in a row, the sun baked down from a cloudless sky. There wasn't any relief from rain or the cool breezes that always came off the lake: pavements became scorching hot. I am emphasizing this because our main street downtown was still a 'yellow-brick road.' The city removed the old bricks years later when they finally got around to paving Franklin Street.

What my ma had forgotten was Huckleberry Finn always went bare-footed. Not only did I skip along, but hopped on one foot then the other for the eight blocks of the parade. I finally had to stop and tie the red bandana on one foot and stick the other foot in the straw hat. It didn't help very much, because they kept falling off. If my ma knew what I was going through, she would have made me quit, but she was three marching bands ahead and had no idea why Huckleberry Finn didn't feel like whistling a happy tune.

Parade officials were waiting at the finish line with two blocks of ice for my feet. While my swollen feet were melting the ice, I could hear the public address system announcing the names of the winners. When I heard Huckleberry Finn and Charlie Chaplin, my feet didn't seem to matter anymore.

It was quite a thrill sitting on the top deck of the enormous ship. We had all the classic Coca-colas and foot-long hot dogs we wanted. I was proud of my ma for creating our winning costumes and she was proud of me for being a true entertainer and finishing the parade. I wondered who it was that coined the phrase, 'the show must go on,' probably a booking agent. It was a special time in my life, sitting up there with my ma and watching the large wake the big steamer was leaving behind. I didn't tell her that my barbequed feet were making me sick to my stomach, especially after she said I was such a super-trooper.

When my ma moved to adjust her chair, Charlie Chaplin's cane slid down and out the railing into the swirling water below. I tried to catch it, but my feet didn't want to move. When the ship reached the fifty-mile distance, it made a big sweeping turn and headed back.

To you it may sound silly, but I had the thought that maybe on the way back we would see that wooden cane floating and somehow recover it.

To get me home, my ma had to carry me piggyback. She

immediately smeared a lotion containing witch hazel on my blisters and wrapped my feet in bandages. I couldn't walk on my own for many days after that. What bothered me the most was she blamed herself for all the suffering I was going through, hopping along the sun-baked 'yellow-brick road.' In the winter months, I spent most nights inside because of the freezing weather after dark. I loved staying up with my ma listening to all the popular radio programs emanating out of the Chicago stations. Our city was only fifty-some miles away and the radio signal always came in strong and clear. Our favorite Saturday night shows were, 'I Love a Mystery'... 'Lights Out'...'The Shadow' and 'The Lone Ranger.' On Sunday night it was the 'First Niters' with Don Ameche and the many comedy shows with the likes of: Red Skeleton...Fibber McGee and Molly...Bob Hope...Jack Benny to name a few. We laughed so hard our sides ached.

When it came to humor, my ma enjoyed a good joke as long as it wasn't racial or sexual. Whenever someone started to tell a joke in my presence, she always monitored the story. If the joke had any sexual overtones to it she would stop the person by holding up her hand and say, 'T.M.I.', which the guy telling the joke would ask, what do you mean, 'T.M.I.?' My ma would cover my ears with her hands and say... 'Too- Much- Information.' That would always bring a laugh even from the person wanting to tell it.

I am going to pause in my story right here and tell you my ma's one and only joke. I must have heard her tell it hundreds of times. It was about this guy who always bragged about what he did or had, was more than anyone else. It got to the point his fellow workers were getting very sick of it. One day as he was expounding on how great his wife could sing, he said, "yesterday at her singing lesson she got up to high C and held it for a whole minute." One of the guys that couldn't take it any longer said, "That's nothing, the other night my wife got up to P...couldn't find the pot and held it all night." Because it was her favorite joke, I never got tired of hearing it.

My ma would make popcorn in a wired meshed basket that she shook back and forth over flames of the gas stove to keep the kernels for scorching. She made enough to fill two sugar kettles and colored the corn with a variety of vegetable colorings, then sprinkled sugar on it. She mixed it in a large wash pan. To this day it is the best tasting popcorn I ever had and the most colorful too.

To make sure we would be cozy and warm over in the living room, she fed Old Lucifer with a full load of coal to get his wrought-iron belly glowing red-hot. With our bowls of popcorn, we sat close to each other on the sofa. My ma liked to turn off the lights. She said it would make the scary shows even scarier and it sure did. What little light there was came from the dial on the Crosley radio and the little windows in the fire door of Old Lucifer. The only sound other than the radio was an occasional snap popping of the exploding coals that raged in the fire. The red glow behind the Mica windows made the stove look like a fiery-eyed dragon. There were many nights as I sat cuddling next to my ma, that I knew she was wishing my father Michael was also sitting with us having popcorn. I wonder if you have the same question in mind that I have. Now that I think of it, if my ma knew we were going to turn off the lights, why bother to color the popcorn?

Chapter 20

In my early years, I seldom went out of the neighborhood, which left me little opportunity to see other nationalities living on God's great earth. My neighbors and town people were all white skinned. The first time I saw a black person, I was in awe of him. It happened on Sunday morning when playing with Snowflake and Curly. They suddenly left me and ran across the yard to greet a man walking past the house. I looked up to see who the dogs were running to and my first thought was to call the dogs back in fear of this strange looking creature. That however ended when I saw them jumping up to lick his face and turn over on their backs allowing him to rub their little pink tummies. I could hear him talking gently to them and showing no signs of being something to fear. I didn't know what else to do, but watch Snowflake and Curly as they welcomed this odd-looking stranger to join in our game.

He was dressed in bib-overalls, long sleeved checkered shirt and wearing a pair of old, but highly shined Army boots. Removing his strange looking cap to say hello, it revealed a head of jet-black fuzzy hair that showed signs of thinning. When he bent over to pet the dogs, I noticed a hump formed on the left side of his back. Looking over at my ma, cutting flowers for our supper table, he was the first to speak.

"Gud mor'n Ma'm, look lac the Law'd

Confederate army kepi

AMERICAN
Most Union soldiers wore a soft cap with a stiffened peak. This type of headgear was called a kepi. Confederate troops wore a gray, broad-brimmed hat or a kepi with a blue band.

has done bless' us wid notha bute'ful day."

Evidently, she was not as concerned about him as I was and walked over to say, "Yes we are having a lot of perfect weekends this summer." From then on, the weather was the start of their conversions when he passed by our house.

He introduced himself as Jethro G. Washington. My ma shook his hand and gave her name. When introducing me, he held out his hand, but I quickly jumped back, hiding mine behind me. He said Washington was the surname his grandfather had chosen when freed from slavery. His reason for coming up north was to get away from all the hate and killing of blacks that was still going on in the southern states. He heard about our beautiful city where the sand was so pure and clean, when you walked along the beach at water's edge, the grains gave out musical tones. The city in its promotional advertising used, "ON THE SHORES OF SINGING SANDS. It was a city also to become famous for its mysterious murders.

Mr. Washington said he was looking for steady employment, some place they could use a hard working laborer from a southern plantation. Another thing that caught my eye was the strange looking cap he wore. Mr. Washington said it was part of a Confederate uniform called a Kepi and that his daddy, along with many other slaves, helped the Confederate army in their fight against the north.

Mr. Washington said his daddy found the Kepi cap on a battlefield and allowed him to keep it. They warned him never to wear it up north. There were southern Rebs that came north, still blaming the blacks for causing the war.

"Ah puts on dah cap wenev'a Ah goes to ma Sunday meet'n at dat lil' church." He told us they held Sunday services in a barn outside of the city limits west of town. He wore that Kepi cap as a proud treasured memory of his daddy. "Ah go'na gets me somp'n else soons Ah gets me mah fus pay."

"Yes, you had better get some new clothes right away, Mr. Washington. Many southern soldiers have moved up here. I don't think they'll like the idea of seeing an ex-slave flaunting the Kepi cap of a Johnny Reb," she informed him.

"Ah no's yo right, Ma'm cuz Ah works wid one dat do grave dig'n wid me. He say, he bettah not kech me wear'n ma daddy's cap roun' 'im or he go'na tar dat cap rat off'n ma black nigga head."

My ma said, "Well I think you better report him to your boss. Maybe he could talk to your co-worker and tell him that the terrible Civil War is over and all of us Americans are trying to get on with our lives."

"O Ah thinks Mist'ah Dugan do talk to dat Mist'ah Melon, but Ah still see's how he look mad at me al'time. Ah don' wanna eva' turn ma back on'm an Ah ain't eva go'na dig graves wid only he'n me out'n dat cem'try."

Dig-it kept the men overtime on many occasions. Their job was to go out in the cemetery and fill in those half-dug graves. We could see them from our porch with their lanterns still working long after the sun had settled in the west.

I asked my ma "was Mr. Washington talking about the Mr. Melon who is renting the apartment next door?"

"Yes you're right, Januschek, one of them is named Melon and his friend's last name is Balan. Both of them came up together from the south. Evidently Mr. Washington isn't having any better luck getting away from the violence in the south."

He told us he was running out of the money his daddy had given him to get started and had been standing in line looking for any type of work he could get. They told him to try the pump-house at the cemetery, because at times they added men whenever there were many funerals listed on the work board.

He said, "Ah lac mah boss man, Mist'ah Dugan, cuz he treats me fine. He say he gonna keep me on dat dig'n crew steady."

"That's wonderful Mr. Washington and then you'll be getting a weekly income and maybe start a family of your own."

"Well, Ahs hop'n to, Mam' but Ah ain't seen but only a few otha black fok's since Ah cum yer. Ah bin think'n mebbe Ah send fur mah wom'n, an she be mah miss's."

PRUSSIAN ARMY TELESCOPE

19th-century Prussian helmet

PRUSSIAN
From about 1835, Prussian soldiers wore helmets with decorative spikes, something the French army adopted after its defeat in the Franco-Prussian War.

SWORD-BREAKER KNIFE

"Where are you living now Mr. Washington, she asked?"

"Ahs liv'n way on da otha side of da city. Mebbe win Ah gets wed, Ah gonna fine me somp'n closa to da cem'try."

"Well, when you are ready to do that, you can come and check out the apartment next door to us and if it is available you'd be welcome to live here," she offered.

I didn't know how the gypsy lady would react to my ma's plan, but I am ashamed to say I bet her crystal ball would not only fog up, but also explode.

Chapter 21

My grandfather had a collection of old army memorabilia, which included a Polish retractable telescope, a Prussian Captain's brass parade helmet and a dagger used way back when battles were still being fought with swords. The Sword Breaker was a unique weapon that had many uses. Made from German steel the blade had razor sharpness. The other side had a serrated edge with spaces wide enough to trap an enemy's sword. It was held in the sword fighters opposite hand and all it took was a twist of the wrist to break off the enemy's blade, leaving him defenseless. My ma kept the Sword Breaker in the kitchen and used it as a butcher knife. It was a great tool for cutting up fruit and vegetables, or carving meat. She used the serrated side for beating the hell out of a tough slab of meat, like round steak. It made it tender as any steak served in high-class restaurants.

I spent many hours playing soldier up in my bedroom. I wore the Captain's helmet, which I had to stuff with paper to keep it from falling over my eyes and pretended I was a handsome Polish officer. The cemetery was the battleground and the hundreds of tombstones were the enemy forces. I guess somewhere deep inside I had a hidden desire to be a brave soldier like my father Martin.

There were times when I had trouble getting to sleep at night, especially the nights before a test at school. I would use the telescope to scan the cemetery grounds. If it was a bright moonlit night, I could watch the animals as they hunted their prey. The cemetery was full of tomcats chasing rabbits in wild pursuit putting on a show that few people ever realized was taking place as they slept through the night. It was interesting to watch them as they wildly darted around and over the tombstones. I was hoping to see a cat and rabbit having sex. I learned this from one of the 'older guys' at the pow-wow. After many weeks of not seeing the act, I made a big no-no by doubting the authenticity of that guy's statement, "How do you know cats and rabbits do it? Have you ever seen them?" He immediately came and stood towering over me. I sat there with my legs crossed looking up at him fearing his next move.

He said, "Hey kid, haven't you ever heard of hare on a pussy?"

The 'older guys' could hardly control their laughter, because they always got such a big kick out of making fools of us. I was too naïve at the time to know why they thought it was so funny, until Snort explained it was just a play on words. Evidently, Snort didn't think it was funny either, because he didn't ride off on his bike laughing and snorting... I really liked Snort.

The most exciting time was when I used the telescope to spy on lovers in the cemetery. I accidentally discovered one night that there were sex orgies taking place after the bars closed on Saturday. In those days, motels had strict laws about unmarried couples renting rooms for the evening. Those restrictions, plus the cost of the room, made them search for hiding places where they could make-out in their cars. I happened upon this by chance one Saturday night watching the animals. As I started scanning the area with my telescope, I noticed a line of little lights moving in the darkness. It took me a while to realize that they were the parking lights of cars entering the cemetery through the main gateway over on Tilden Street. I kept watching as they slowly entered and spread out in different directions to park among the tombstones and bushes. By staying behind the shrubbery, they hid from the police at ground level, as they circled the cemetery. Aha, but at a two-story level it was a different ballgame. With the powerful lens of the telescope and the angle from my window, I could focus right down on the cars. Although the distance was nearly a hundred yards or so, the power of the lens made me feel as if I was standing on the car's running board. Back then, that was a convenient step for getting in and out of a car. The windows were a lot smaller than the cars of today, but I could still detect heads kissing and bare dupas. Some even got out of their cars to spread blankets on the graves. I couldn't help but think of the threatening line, "Not over my dead body!" The best viewing of all was when they hopped into the rumble seat.

With the sight of all that sex, the aching started in my groin and as usual, I ended up doing my peepka routine. There was always a feeling of shame that came over me as I lay in bed staring up at the ceiling thinking how disappointed my ma would be if she discovered my secret. What eased any feelings of guilt was, I never touched my peepka with my hands and there was never any wetness from the contractions either. It wasn't me, but the people in the cemetery that were doing all the sinning. Guilty or not, I couldn't wait till the next Saturday, hoping there would be another full moon to light up the stage for the fornicating thespians.

Chapter 22

O ne kid seemed out of place in my neighborhood. Wilbur Weidendorf was four years older, but always hung around us kids. I often wondered why he didn't join in with the 'older guys.' Not only was he older, but also you could see by his muscles he was a prime candidate for a future body builder. Although Wilbur at times showed a tendency to be a little on the bully side, he never acted that way toward me. I think he admired me, because I was so good at sports and he didn't have any coordination at all. His forte was building go-carts out of orange crates or re-assembling bicycles from old parts from the city dump. Whenever he used his father's ten-pound sledgehammer, knocking frames back in shape, you could hear the clanging all over the neighborhood.

It was puzzling why Wilbur never had a butch haircut, but always wore his hair shoulder-length even in the hot days of summer. With his muscle-bound body and shoulder-length hair, something just did not fit. His arms not only had bulging muscles, but those muscles had muscles. The first time I saw them, I thought they were monkey-bumps that never went back down.

I started to pal around with him only because he gave me transportation on the frame of his bike. For instance, out to the pier for a day of fishing or to the swimming-hole for skinny-dipping. In fact, Wilbur talked me into going skinny-dipping in the first place. I guess at the swimming-hole I was always so engrossed in the fun I was having, I did not realize how strange Wilbur acted. I started to notice he was always right behind me and at times pushed me to the ground. He ended up on top of me, laughing as if it was just a joke. At first, I thought it was his rough way of having fun. He kept asking me to come with him on the other side of the bushes. I couldn't see what fun we could have over there out of the water, so I asked Snort. He said, "Michael, remember what I told you about girls, who like to have sex with boys?" "Yes I do, Snort." "Well, there are boys who like to have sex with boys." With that statement, he snorted out of sight, leaving me wondering how much more complicated can life get.

Chapter 23

It was early on a Saturday morning in December, one of the worst tragedies of my young life occurred. It had snowed through the night, so I had to walk on the road to Stash's Tavern. About a block up from the house, I noticed a patch of red on the snow bank. To me it looked like a scarf had fallen out of some car and the plow threw it up on the bank. When I saw what it was, I almost fainted and stood completely stunned. There on the bank laid the body of the sweetest little dog that God ever created. With trembling hands, I picked up the limp body of Snowflake. The shock left me so weak I sank to my knees and screamed, "NO, NO, OH MY GOD, NO!"

It took awhile for me to regain my composure and carry Snowflake to show Stash. It was going to be a tremendous blow to that big guy who adored Snowflake so dearly. When I was about a block and a half from the bar, I saw a brown spot on the snow bank ahead. Oh, my God this couldn't be happening. No God, no I cried...not Curly too! Yes, it was Curly. He was also lying up on the bank covered with patches of blood.

Now there were two of the sweetest animals ever put on this earth in my arms and I was taking them to break the heart of the nicest human on earth. I wondered if Stash would ever be able to get over this devastating loss.

As I neared the bar, I saw him shoveling the walk. He had his back to me and I could hardly get the words out of my mouth.

"Stash, look what I found." Recognizing the sound of my voice, he turned to give me his usual ear-to-ear smile. At first, his eyes didn't focus on what I was carrying until I held my arms up to him. When he saw the dogs, his massive shoulders drooped and he turned as white as the snow he was clearing. I can still hear the loud yell Stash made as he flung the snow shovel clear across Barker Avenue. Taking the dogs from me, he slumped down on the steps. His large body went into convulsions as he shouted, "Sweet Jesus why...why...why? The two of us sat there on the tavern steps for what seemed like hours. While I tried my best to console him, he kept rocking back and forth, shedding tears on his lifeless little pets. It choked me up so much it felt like a rock was stuck in my throat. I could hardly swallow, let alone try to offer words to ease his suffering. With my hands on his shoulders, we rocked and cried together.

Realizing that customers would soon be arriving, Stash stood up and said, "I have to take Snowflake and Curly out in back and clean them up. I won't need your help Michael, but if you want to stay and work you can."

"Gee Stash; I am so sick I just want to go home. Is that all right?"

"I understand Michael and when you feel up to working again you can come back." I was so emotionally drained all I wanted to do was go home and lay down. I even had hopes of waking to find Snowflake and Curly licking my face and find the terrible tragedy was just a nightmare.

By the time I arrived home, the remains of my breakfast were along the snowy path to our front door and all I had left were dry heaves. I immediately went up to my bedroom and prayed to God. I told him that there would soon be two wonderful little dogs named

Snowflake and Curly arriving to romp and play in his beautiful heaven. I know they will be excited to show you what they learned here on earth. God, just say...trick.

Stash and I racked our brains to come up with an answer of how it must have happened. His theory was he had gotten a call from his lawyer with an offer on the property west of the tavern. Because of its growing popularity, Stash needed more room for parking. He and the owner had been dickering back and forth for many months. The lawyer called and said the seller was ready to take his offer and he and Hilda should come to the office immediately to strike while the iron was hot. Stash had a suitcase he kept all his business documents in and ready to go at any time. He forgot that Snowflake and Curly were playing out behind the bar. He thought the dogs saw him jump into the car with the suitcase. To them it must have looked like we were going on another vacation. Thinking they were supposed to go to your house to be doggie-sat, they headed down Barker Avenue.

I thought his theory made a lot of sense, but how did they die? Did a car hit them and if so, why were their bodies found so far apart? The big question I had was, what were the dogs doing out in the street anyway? Stash trained them never to go off the sidewalk. What was also odd, each dog had the same death causing injury. Both Snowflake and Curly had their throats torn away. Could it have been a car... a snowplow, or maybe... a jealous animal named, Dupa?

Chapter 24

There weren't any pet cemeteries back then, maybe in New York, but not in our little town. I am sure Stash would have taken a plot for his dogs, if any were available. I asked if I could help make the gravesite and was so excited when he agreed... I couldn't wait to get started. Stash came up with a great idea. He took two pony beer kegs, cut them in half, cemented the inside and put hinges on the top pieces to make little caskets. He said he was planning to bury the dogs in the back of the bar, out by the hedges that lined the alley and then surround the monument with a vine-covered trellis, bent in a cove-shape to create a shrine effect. I wanted to help him with everything, but he said the headstone would be too heavy for me and he was strong enough to do it himself.

I told him it would work out fine, because my ma and I would be visiting my aunt and uncle in Chicago. Steve had a job interview with a newly formed company and after that, we would be staying in their rented five bedroom, three-bath home. I don't know why they would need three baths; one was sufficient for our house and maybe someday it would even have hot running water.

Upon arriving back from Chicago, I immediately threw my suitcase on the bed, raced out the front door and up the two blocks to the tavern. I ran past the customers, out the back door, got halfway across the yard and stopped dead in my tracks by the sight of a beautiful little shrine. There was not a grave in Greenwood Cemetery that was more elaborate. If people ever wondered how much Stash loved his Snowflake and Curly, all they had to do was look at that shrine. I used the sleeve of my jacket to wipe away the tears that formed in my eyes. Stash must have seen me running through the bar, because he immediately came out to get my reaction. "Well, what do you think Michael?"

"Stash, it's breathtaking," I wanted to say more, but choked up and couldn't continue. The headstone was made of very expensive close-grained blue granite. It measured three feet high by three feet wide and sat on a four-inch thick base. I thought at the time it was a little big for a pet headstone, but Stash's heart was big and the headstone just proved it. The epitaph read...In memory of Snowflake and Curly...Love Stash

Chapter 25

One Thursday night I wished I hadn't taken the telescope to look out in the cemetery. The moon lit up the grounds like a major league ballpark. I just had to take one quick look before going to bed. While scanning across the area I passed two people on a blanket. At the time, I thought it was rather strange seeing lovers in the cemetery on a weeknight, but I figured as long as the couple was out there for me to watch...why not. I brought my lens back and zeroed in. I could see that the female had blond hair and was completely naked except for her shoes. I didn't get a good look at their faces until they finished and sat up to light a cigarette. The glow of the lighter afforded me a clear description of the pair. At the shock of recognizing the couple, I almost dropped the telescope out the window. I just couldn't believe what I was seeing and wished I never had. The blond woman was Stash's wife Hilda and the guy was my stepfather Frank.

After putting the telescope away, I climbed in bed and lay staring up at the ceiling completely stunned. My brain kept rerunning the scene I had just witnessed. I knew then, the rumor that Hilda was fooling around was now a fact. I was afraid of what Frank would do to me if I told him I watched as he auditioned for her so called... 'the right man.' From that time on, I struggled with the problem of telling my ma what I discovered. I decided it would only add more frustration to her already disgusting marriage and my episodes with the telescope would end forever.

Chapter 26

W hen the city received its official charter in 1836, the only warning at the harbor's mouth was merely a lantern on top of a metal post at the water's edge. By the time my grandfather arrived, it was replaced with Government Pier running north on Lake Michigan to a lighthouse that towered over seventy feet. The ships could see its beam all the way from

Chicago. To withstand the pounding giant waves formed by tempest storms, the base of the tower had huge cement boulders protecting it. You could hear the foghorn from a twenty-mile radius. When it was in use, people in town had to shout over it to be heard. The weather forecasting back then wasn't as technical as it is today; sudden unexpected storms destroyed many boats and lives were lost. One of which was a very popular sports writer for our local paper, who also had many featured articles in national sports magazines.

The worst nautical disaster took place in 1933 and claimed the lives of four commercial tugboat workers. Two boats set out to work their nets. One was the forty-five foot tugboat Martha and the other was the Dad Ludwig. The weather that morning had a strange and eerie calmness about it. Before the tugs could reach their destination, a sudden change in wind direction caused them to turn back. The barometers that morning were not forecasting any bad weather but sudden wind changes were bad omens. Whenever one of those unpredictable storms hit the area, many vessels struggled to make it back into the haven of the harbor. The local radio station would immediately interrupt its regular programming to give running detailed accounts on the boats in trouble. It didn't take very long for the lakefront to fill up with local citizens climbing up the sand dunes with their blankets and binoculars. My ma never went as a spectator before, but this time there was a chance Frank and Dupa could be on one of those boats. Frank had taken the cat with him that week to get rid of the persistent rodents that were ravaging the food supply. My ma suggested going right down on the beach, so she could be near the tragedy and pray for the safe return of the tugs. I had mixed emotions about praying for Frank, who would only come back and torment her. I felt ashamed when I realized she was not just praying for him.

By the time we arrived at Washington Park, there were not many parking places left. I could see hundreds of sightseers had already perched themselves high up on the sand dunes, to watch the drama unfold. I remembered that the best place to view the action would be at the city's landmark and logo building, The Observation Tower. I told my ma I was taking the telescope to view the action.

With her Bible tucked under her arm, my ma immediately headed straight to where the angry waves were relentlessly crashing on shore. I ran as fast as I could to the tower and without stopping, climbed the two hundred and twenty steps to the top. It was surprising to find I was the only one up there. I quickly pulled out the sections of the telescope and with my shirttail wiped off the lens to get the clearest picture possible.

Viewing the lake from that high perch, I had to fight the urge to pretend I was in the crow's nest of an English naval ship, scanning the horizon for the terrible pirate, Captain Kidd. When I zoomed in on the action taking place beyond the lighthouse, I was amazed how clear the view was. They called it a sudden blow and it came from the north, with straight-line winds reported to have reached over sixty miles an hour.

The name on the first boat I sighted was the Martha. She was coming from the northeast at full throttle. She was only a few hundred feet from the mouth of the harbor. When she made her turn to come around the lighthouse to safety, a huge wave slammed into her side. It shoved the tug sideways into the choppy waters. I didn't see her again until she attempted to come around the west side of the lighthouse. The tug suddenly swung around a hundred and eighty degrees and started back out the way she came in.

It was reported later that the Martha had a broken rudder cable, leaving her helplessly floundering around in the angry waters. To add to that problem, another wave ripped through the cabin and sent it crashing against the boulders at the base of the lighthouse.

There were men out in the water clinging to pieces of wreckage and another man at the base of the pier desperately hanging on to the corner of a cement boulder. The strong wind was now blowing rain horizontally and blurred the lens of my telescope. I wasn't quite sure, but the man clinging for dear life looked a lot like Frank. I had to get a better look, so I stopped to clean the lens. When I zeroed back in to the base of the lighthouse, the man was sliding down out of sight into the swirling water.

The pilothouse of the Martha finally wound up west of the Government's breaker pier. They found the wreckage way over to the east or lakeside of the harbor. The coast guard could only retrieve the steering wheel and four unused life jackets of the doomed craft.

A later editorial commenting on the storm, stated that not just one person was to blame; it is the fault of all who have let the harbor become shallow by sewage, refuge and a thick layer of silt; which in a heavy sea is always a bad situation.

Captain Henry Newberry of the Dad Ludwig reporting on the storm told of a strange thing that occurred. He said his vessel and the Martha were both on their way out to the nets, when they felt a sudden gust of wind. From years of experience, they feared it could possibly develop into a gale. Each decided to turn around and start back to the safety of the harbor. The ill-fated Martha took the lead and reached the entrance first. The Dad Ludwig only a few knots behind, had no knowledge of the disaster that had just taken place ahead of them. The lighthouse attendant reported that by the time the second tug entered the area, the lake suddenly and mysteriously returned to calmness, acting like it had nothing to do with the four bodies that lay up on the cement boulders of the lighthouse.

While I was watching the disaster taking place, I remembered that I didn't ask my ma the name of the tug Frank worked on. I found out later when he showed up at the house with Dupa, he was on the second boat, the Dad Ludwig. When they interviewed Frank's crew, not one of them had any idea why they came out of the incident unscathed. Frank believed it was because he had his lucky rabbit's foot Dupa with him.

I had my own theory...What about all the prayers my saintly mother said on the beach?

Chapter 27

Even though our city was small in population, it had a superb coast guard. So superb, that during World War II, the U.S. government used it to train new recruits. The vast amount of open water for ship maneuvering and the only functional lighthouse on all of Lake Michigan made it an ideal area for basic training. There was also the experience of precise steering through the sharp turn in the harbor's channel to the ship's final dockage.

Although there were only a dozen or so trainees at a time, many came from neighborhoods in big cities where the youth grew up in different environments. Their lack of respect for city ordinances and complete indifference to sexual behavior was upsetting our peaceful law-abiding citizens to no end. It seemed that the sight of a sailor uniform and a cocked sailor hat, made the teenage girls go bonkers over them. The young and vibrant sailors gave the town quite a problem. They were impregnating the naïve high school girls. There were so many citizens storming City Hall to complain about their wild behavior, that the mayor wrote Washington demanding some restrictions. It must have made an impact on the admirals, because the local paper had an article on the front page stating some changes at the coast guard station. They built eight-foot high cyclone fences around the area and added restrictions to stop the young studs from going into town at night.

According to the 'older guys' at the pow-wow, the new restrictions didn't help a bit. Girls were still having sex late at night with their hot-blooded idols. Even though they turned the lighting off in the area, the swooning bobby-sockers were still sneaking up to the fence to rendezvous with their worldly boyfriends. In spite of the fence separating them, they were still finding ways to perform the sex act. The guys said the girl positioned herself at the opening of the square in the cyclone fence, proving the old adage..."where there's a will there's a way." It may sound a bit ironic, but there was even a hit song at the time by Bing Crosby called, "Don't Fence Me In," or to quote the famous boxer Joe Lewis, "If you see an opening... take it."

The problem ended after World War II. The sexy Navy uniforms were replaced with a new craze... the Zoot Suit.

Remember I promised I would not pull any punches but tell it the way I heard or experienced it. By the way, just in case you are wondering... the square in the fence measures two and a quarter by two and a quarter.

Chapter 28

My ma always wanted to send me to a Catholic school, but could never afford the tuition. With the influx of money coming from her paper hanging and costume business, plus rent money received from Aunt Helen and Uncle Steve, made it a little more affordable. After I finished the sixth grade at Marsh Elementary, my ma enrolled me at St. Mary's Catholic High School. She said because I didn't understand Polish, it would be easier for me to study the Catechism in English. I found out that because of my late start, I would be the oldest kid receiving the sacraments.

It was common knowledge how the nuns ran their classes. The report was strictly business and absolutely no fooling around. I also heard that on certain occasions there could be a light tap on the knuckles with a ruler. It was very different from the treatment that the principal at Marsh Elementary administered. When he substituted for a teacher, he never used a ruler to control a student. His technique was to casually walk around to the back of the room and come down the aisle of the unsuspecting kid. When passing by he would give the kid a slap on the side of his face with the back of his hand. What made it painful was the ring he wore. It had a huge Cameo setting that at times cut the student's cheek. I don't know how true it was, but a kid at the pow-wow said the inscription read… MOM.

Parents had a different view of teachers back then, especially principals. They put them on a pedestal, so to speak and seldom reprimanded them. In today's circumstances however, they would handle it differently.

Going to another school meant I would have to travel a good two and a half miles to the other side of town. There weren't school buses picking up city kids, so you had to walk or find some other means of transportation. My ma solved that problem with a gift for my upcoming first communion. It was a beautiful Sears and Roebuck bicycle with white-rimmed balloon tires and all the other accessories added. She gave me the bike so I could learn to ride it by the time school started. It gave me transportation in the fall and summer, but was of little use on the icy, unsalted streets. I still had to walk five miles a day toting my adult lunch bucket, plus all the homework that the nuns gave me.

I will never forget the shock of getting an A+ in history my first semester. I have to thank my ma for that. She handed me an American history book that belonged to my grandfather. He used it to study for his American citizenship papers. She even dog-eared the chapter for me. I wrote an essay on the subject of blacks during the Civil War and copied the text, word for word. I was surprised to learn, although the slaves formed a regiment of their own, the south wouldn't issue them confederate uniforms. The slaves weren't the only blacks that fought in the war. President Lincoln also decided to use black troops even though many whites believed that blacks would make poor soldiers. About 180 thousand blacks served in the Union army. Two-thirds of them were southern slaves who had fled to freedom in the North. Twenty thousand black sailors also served in the Union Navy. There were 166 all-black regiments, most of which had white commanders. Only about 100 blacks made officer. Blacks fought in nearly 500 Civil War engagements, including 39 major battles where thousands of black service men lost their lives. Altogether, 23 blacks won the Medal of Honor, America's highest military award for heroism. A black regiment was one of the first northern armies to march into Richmond after it fell. When Lincoln toured the city, black soldiers escorted him.

At first, black soldiers received only about half the pay of white soldiers. In 1864, Congress finally granted blacks equal pay. The south objected strongly to the north using black soldiers. The southern Confederate government threatened to kill or enslave any captured enlisted men of black regiments. Lincoln in return promised to treat Confederates the same way. Neither side carried out those threats, however.

After reading that segment, I could see why my ma never had the apprehension I did when seeing Mr. Washington that first day. I had a mother that absolutely harbored no prejudice against any race or religion. To her, all humans were God's wonderful creation. From then on, I could not wait to run up and offer my hand to Mr. Washington. However, I never got the opportunity to atone for my rudeness. His visits on Sunday suddenly stopped.

Chapter 29

I also remember when it came time for first confession, I was supposed to give thought to the sins I could remember. My ma said she wanted me to have a good soul-clearing revelation and God would forgive me. My biggest problem was remembering a sin. I guess I could have made some up by saying God's name in anger a few times, or that I had missed Sunday Mass once, but that would be lying to the Priest. I didn't steal anything, so the only sins left were sexual and that was questionable too. My ma said it was a sin if I found enjoyment touching my peepka or doing nasty things with those 'Shoestring girls.' In my mind, I never thought I would ever have sex sins. I suppose the act of watching the lovers in the cemetery could qualify as a sin, but I wasn't the one committing the act. My gratification didn't come from touching my peepka with my hands either. It was between my legs. I didn't have the slightest idea what I would confess. I kept soul searching for something that could be a sin, when I remembered the time my ma bought me a Roy Rogers cap gun. She wouldn't let me have anything more dangerous than that on the Fourth of July. She also bought two boxes of caps, which didn't take me long to use up. In fact, they were gone two days before the Fourth. I just couldn't resist shooting out my bedroom window at the charging Prussian army. I felt very brave wearing my beautiful Captain's helmet and sighting the enemy through my German telescope. I don't think I missed a single tombstone soldier.

It was on July 3 while playing outside that I saw a girl named Teresa. She lived a few blocks from my home up Cloud Street. She was in my class at school, but I never had playtime with any of the kids from her neighborhood. They had their own gang. I knew she liked me by the way she acted at school. My ma told me to watch out for girls that flirted and lured boys to do naughty things. The 'older guys' told us the same thing. They said when they were our age, girls were always asking them to play house. That is how they left it...'play house.' If it weren't for Snort, I would never have learned what went on when you played house. He said, "Michael, what do you think? They're the wife and you're the husband." Snort again left me before I could ask my other question, which would have been, what are the naughty things they do? I don't think Snort would have known himself or that he ever played house.

When Teresa heard me clicking the trigger of my cap less gun she said her brother had many caps and would I like a box?

I said, "Boy would I ever, but I don't have any money Teresa."

"You don't need any money Michael. I'll give you a box for your doctor's fee." "My doctor's fee, what's that?"

"It's what I will pay you for playing doctor with me." I remembered what Snort told me...she is the wife and you are the husband, but this is not the same thing, I thought. My role this time would be that of a respected doctor, not a husband. I thought maybe Teresa would be the nurse and we would be curing little babies using her dolls as patients. I convinced myself there was nothing naughty and I really wanted to show my ma that I still had caps for celebrating the Fourth. I told Teresa I would do it, but only for a little while.

"Oh great," she beamed. "Come over to my house, we have a pup tent in our back yard and we'll use it for the operating room."

An operating room I wondered. Why did we need an operating

room? What was I getting into? Was she luring me into breaking one of God's commandments? All the way over to Teresa's house I had a bad feeling about the situation, but the idea of free caps kept urging me on. At least I thought it was the caps.

When we arrived in Teresa's back yard, I saw the pup tent where the nurse and doctor were going to pretend to cure little babies. What a surprise I had when the very moment we entered the tent, Teresa laid down on her belly, raised up her skirt and slid down her panties. She immediately said, "what's wrong with me doctor?" I was in complete shock as I stared down at a girl's bare dupa for the first time. I remembered thinking how it didn't look any different from the boys at the swimming hole. I was completely dumfounded and had no idea what she expected me to do. I said, "What do I do now Teresa?"

She said, "Kneel down and pretend you are examining me." Examining her for what I wondered. I never heard of nurses having sick dupas. I knew I shouldn't touch her with my hands, because that would certainly be sinning. I had to think fast, so I looked around and found a discarded Popsicle stick. I planned to use it as an instrument, make a few quick probes, take my caps and get the heck out of that hospital. I told Teresa there wasn't anything I could find wrong with her and started to get up from my knees, when she ordered me not to stop. "You haven't earned your doctor's fee yet Michael." While deciding what else I could do to earn my caps, I got a great idea. I thought this was a perfect chance to find out what a girl looks like between her legs. I knew if I just looked and didn't touch, it wouldn't be committing a sin. Therefore, I said, "Teresa, maybe I could find something wrong with you on the other side." I didn't know if she planned on going any further then letting me examine her dupa, until I saw her turning to lie on her back. The excitement that was building up in me came to a sudden stop when I heard a female voice calling out..."Ter-e-e-sa." When she heard that, she jumped up, pulled up her panties and smoothed out her skirt. She then rushed out of the pup tent leaving me holding my...probing tool. The voice we heard was her mother calling Teresa in for lunch.

While I knelt there wondering when it would be safe to leave, the flap of the pup tent opened and a brand new box of caps came sailing in. I couldn't help but wonder if this was any indication, that little Teresa was well on her well way to becoming a future 'Shoestring.'

The episode made me realize that my childhood was changing. No matter how hard I tried after that, I couldn't erase the sight of a girl's naked dupa. Although I was the innocent victim of an entrapment, guilt and shame engulfed me. I had mixed emotions wondering why I felt more excited about Teresa, than the box of caps I carried in my hand.

Chapter 30

Although I spent hours fishing on Lake Michigan, one incident stands out in my memory. My ma, Aunt Helen, Uncle Steve and I planned to spend all day Sunday fishing and picnicking on Government Pier. We always took a transistor radio to listen to the ball games emanating out of Chicago. My ma and Aunt Helen were Cub fans and Uncle Steve and I liked the White Sox. We drew straws to determine which game to hear. The women were in charge of the food preparation and Uncle Steve and I,

the fishing equipment. My ma said we could all go to Mass on Saturday night, because the church was holding a special Mass for those planning Sunday morning activities.

People came from many cities to fish off that pier, including Chicago. When we arrived at the bait-house, there was a sign saying, SOLD OUT. There was over an hour wait for the truck to return with a new supply. The man said the word must have gotten around that the fish were coming closer to shore and are very active. He said there were so many people fishing, that he sold out in less than an hour. When the minnows did arrive, the price was ten cents a dozen.

For years, you didn't need a license to fish in Lake Michigan.

There were no restrictions on how many poles or bait you could use. When the fish were hungry, they bit at everything. There was one time when I ran out of minnows that I took a little pearl button off my shirt and used it instead. My equipment was a fourteen-foot bamboo pole, a four-foot catgut lead with three Eagle Claw hooks. I spaced them about a foot apart. That was standard for most who fished off the pier. You could wear yourself out in no time at all, pulling up triple-headers, one right after the other. That wonderful body of water furnished thousands of needy people with their evening meals during the depression years.

There was no limit to how many fish you could take home either. When they were hungry, you caught them by the hundreds. Neighbor shared with neighbor and most taverns all over town offered free fish fry dinners to lure customers.

Never in our wildest dreams did we believe this wouldn't go on forever, or that our lake was dying and someday all those fish would be gone. There is a saying that goes like this, "don't mess with Mother Nature" and that is exactly what man did. He changed the topography of the earth by creating a passageway called The St. Lawrence Seaway. It allowed shipments of merchandise from the Atlantic Ocean down into the Great Lakes. They believed that through the years, oceanic marine life infiltrated our fresh water lakes and changed their natural balance. Little did we know that while enjoying our beautiful lake, someday the fisheries with their tugs would go out of business. If Frank had used grandfather's loan to go into the commercial fishing business, he would have lost it all. According to the city's historical records, the phenomenon that occurred went something like this:

There were two Atlantic Ocean infiltrators. The first was the parasitic sea Lamprey, an eel-like water animal with a sucking mouth and no jaw. It was the prime villain in the elimination of the once abundant trout and white fish. The second culprit was a fish of the Herring family called an Alewife. It was the favorite food for trout and whitefish and that kept the population of the Alewife in check. With the Lamprey eliminating the lake trout and white fish, the Alewife population exploded. A study of the lake estimated that at one time, a hundred and seventy-five billion Alewives were in Lake Michigan... Let me repeat, I said, 175 billion. 175,000,000,000

Lakeshore residents awoke one morning with the nauseating stench from millions of dead Alewives that had washed up on the beaches. It was as if the lake couldn't stomach them any longer and puked them up. Our beautiful beach was a stinking mess. The obnoxious odor was even too much for the Sea Gulls, who were scavengers of the lakeshores and they sought food at a more pleasant atmosphere.

A crew of one hundred and eight job corpsmen, established

headquarters for a five-day clean up. The mayor even suggested the use of a flame-thrower to cope with the Alewife beach assault. Although at the time the Alewives were public enemy number one, they became a prime participant in a dramatic project to revive the lake. That is where the Coho Salmon comes in.

Researchers had found a chemical to bring the Lampreys under control. The only problem ensuing from that decision was, as they eliminated the Lampreys, Alewives were free to breed and multiply.

The state of Michigan attempted a wild calculated gamble and established a large-scale salmon fishery in fresh water. They selected the Coho Salmon for a sporting fish that would survive in Lake Michigan. They are short lived, but fast growing, fun to catch and delicious. They also feed voraciously on Alewives. The imaginative venture was beyond everyone's wildest dream. They discovered that salmon would not only thrive in Lake Michigan, but also be self-sustaining and choose to do their spawning in its river systems, Trail Creek being one of them. Whenever the Coho returned to spawn and die, the average size exceeded ten pounds and because of their gorging on Alewives, many had grown in sixteen months to over twenty pounds.

Excitement and hope generated new ideas, innovations and actions on all areas of the lake. Indiana's Department of Natural Resources assigned a salmon specialist and purchased a research vessel for aquatic studies. To establish spawning runs in Hoosier waters, they built a million-dollar cold-water hatchery at Kingsbury, Indiana. They have since added stockings of Chinook, Steelhead, Lake Trout and Brown Trout. The calculated gamble paid off and fishing in Lake Michigan once again is a great sport.

Dale Burgess of the Associated Press concluded that this Coho Salmon explosion is the most exciting thing that has happened to Northwestern Indiana sportsmen since the building of the Government Pier. Charter boats and other facilities are now available to the annual invasion of sport fishermen. The exciting revival of fishing in the lake coincided happily with the emergence of pleasure boating and further clean up and beautification of Trail Creek with added facilities for more boaters.

The outlook for our great lake became brighter than ever. My city with its famous singing sands was now the Coho capital of the Midwest.

Oh, I am sorry...I jumped a few years ahead of my story; so let me continue about our picnic that Sunday.

When we finally made it out on the pier, we were faced with the problem of whether there would be enough room for us to cast out the lines. To give you somewhat of an idea how many people were fishing, the pier was about a quarter mile long and had two sides that you could fish on. They called the east side the lakeside, the west side the harbor side. That made two sides a quarter of a mile long. It took Uncle Steve to calculate how many people would be fishing side by side for a half a mile. I don't remember the exact total, but it was well over three hundred.

We finally squeezed in a small space at the start of the pier. It was the shallow part of the lake and most of the bigger fish preferred deeper water. The space that was available to us was on the harbor side. I never liked that side. I preferred the lakeside out near the lighthouse, but late arrivers had little choice. Our arrangement for fishing positions was that I sat on the left, and then Uncle Steve, Aunt

Helen and my ma would be on the far right. We liked to fish on weekends because the tugs would not be going back and forth creating waves that disrupted the true action of our bobbers and scaring away the many schools of fish. During the week, tugboats were going back and forth with runs to their five hundred gill nets; each a football field long.

There were three companies: Ludwig, Furnas and Ratter. They worked the lake twelve months a year by continually busting through the ice that was forming on the way out to their nets. If for some reason the ice took longer to cut through, the fish could only survive for five to six days. If in the summer, stormy weather kept them from getting out to their nets, hundreds of pounds of beautiful fish spoiled.

The Coast Guard helped the tugs whenever needed. The Dad Ludwig was the largest tug with the most experience. One of her rescue missions was in a storm to pick up a pilot clinging to his downed plane a few miles off the shores of Sheridan Beach. They got the pilot onto the tug, hooked a line to the plane and towed it into the harbor. Port authorities discovered that the plane was full of illegal Canadian whiskey. The pilot was making daily trips from Windsor Canada, to Chicago for the notorious Al Capone.

Although the tugs interrupted the fishing, the crews were friendly and waved their caps shouting, "Ahoy," and some even gave a salute. It was a much-needed industry for our city and we didn't mind the occasional interruptions.

As I sat watching for my next bite, I noticed a strange thing slowly floating past my bobber. The current was carrying it out the harbor from Trail Creek. When the white object got a little closer, I could see that it was a condom. I knew all about rubbers or raincoats as the 'older guys' called them and what they were used for. I was amazed at the length of one, as it came drifting by. His pickle must have turned into a link of Polish sausage. The ring and most of the top portion of the condom was floating on top of the water and the heavier tip hung down just below the surface.

There were so many used rubbers drifting by, it looked like a fleet of merchant ships carrying their load of D.N.A. to dump in deeper waters. So help me, the perch were going wild in a frenzied attack at the lower portion of the condom, thinking it would be something tasty.

I knew it wouldn't take too many more strikes before the tip would break and release its contents. A ridiculous thought crossed my mind; maybe that's how mermaids are created.

I knew my ma spotted them when she pulled up her line and said, "Come on, Januscheck, we're going over on the lakeside because the fish are bigger over there." I knew why she wanted to get me on the other side and I knew by my Uncle Steve's wink, that he also knew. While we were over on the lakeside, another thought crossed my mind. Could it be that Frank was once the proud owner of one of those used condoms? After all, last night was Saturday night and he had never spent a Saturday night at home yet.

It was a good thing those old sailors were smart enough to protect themselves from contacting gonorrhea or syphilis. Those were two of the sexually transmitted diseases of that era. The downtown bars on Saturday nights filled with 'Shoestrings' infected with those dreaded germs. The cure for Gonorrhea at that time was an antibiotic drug called penicillin. A few shots in the cheek of your dupa and the symptoms were gone. It was so easy to get rid of, the 'older guys' laughed about it. They called it 'the Clap.' They even made statements like; you ain't a man, kid, until you have had a dose of 'the Clap.' They also had a name for a girl that was known to have it. She was a 'Clapper.' Back then it had nothing to do with a lighting device.

That was back in my youth. Today it has again become a very serious situation. They never eradicated gonorrhea and syphilis. In fact, today they are on the rise again. Treatment for gonorrhea is more difficult, because the germ is building up a resistance to our current antibiotics. Another great concern is that syphilis increases three to five-fold the risk of acquiring H.I.V., the virus that causes A.I.D.S. The problem is spreading in epic proportions all over the world. Health articles are constantly reminding people that the surest way to avoid the disease is to abstain from having unprotected sex. Another way is to be in a long-term mutually monogamous relationship with a partner who has been tested and known to be uninfected. The third way is to do what those tugboat guys were doing...use the raincoats.

There was a warning to men going into single bars; be careful what you pick up, it may be hot. The same could be true for women; there are studs in the bar that are flirting and boozing, while dicks in their pants are burning and oozing. I thought I would throw in a little poetry.

I was concerned about Frank passing the disease on to my ma, but what I gathered from hints made by Aunt Helen, they never consummated the marriage.

Chapter 31

The news that my Aunt Helen and Uncle Steve were permanently moving to Chicago was quite devastating to us. Uncle Steve had been making periodic trips to Chicago for interviews with a relatively new company dealing with agricultural products. It had something to do with farming and husbandry. He heard the company was to grow nationwide and even had their sights on international offices.

Uncle Steve with his God-given gift for mathematics was to head the bookkeeping department. He said it was a great opportunity to get in on the ground floor of a promising young company and as the business grew; he would grow along with it. As it turned out, his dream about the company came true in just ten years. They promoted him through the growth years and soon he was the head-honcho of the company's multi-million dollar bookkeeping department.

Aunt Helen and Uncle Steve's first house was on the outskirts of Chicago. It was a moderate building in a low-income neighborhood located twenty miles from his work. As the years went by, they kept buying larger homes closer to his office. They finally settled into a house designed to their specifications. The property was only three miles from his place of employment. In fact, so close, Uncle Steve never bothered driving his expensive car, but would put on his jogging clothes and run the three miles to work. His office included a full shower, in addition; a walk-in closet with several changes of business suits. He said the jogging gave him a chance to breathe fresh air to help clear his mind for the many bookkeeping problems that occurred throughout his working hours. At the end of his long day, he would reverse the whole process and jog back home.

Although we were happy for them, it meant that my ma and I would be the only ones living at home. The apartment next to us was now vacant, which meant no rent payments every month. Where there once was a grandfather, aunt, uncle and an absentee husband, now lived just two people... an eight-year old boy with his devoted mother.

My aunt and uncle invited us at least a couple times a year. We rode the South Shore electric train that ran from South Bend, Indiana, through our town and all the way some fifty miles to Chicago. It was my first time on a train. We sat up in the observation car and watched the beautiful scenery as it rapidly passed by. Whenever we went by a farm with a herd of cows, my ma would turn and state a number. When I asked her what the number stood for she said, "I'm counting the amount of cows in each herd."

I said, "Ma, how can you do that when we're going by so fast? You're even quicker at math than Uncle Steve."

"Oh it's easy, Januscheck, I just count the number of legs and divide by four." She also told me that snowflakes are snowmen unassembled. My ma really had a great sense of humor.

The first few years Uncle Steve would come and pick us up at the station, but in later years, he had a limo waiting. They liked taking us on tours of the big city, which included the downtown loop with all of the tall skyscrapers. I still remember how dizzy I got standing in awe looking up to the top of the building, which seemed to me were swaying a little. We dined at famous loop restaurants and took in shows at beautiful theaters that were still featuring vaudeville acts.

Before we left for home, we learned some startling facts and information about Frank. Aunt Helen never was satisfied with his reluctance to talk about the past. She wanted to hire a private detective, but during the depression, there wasn't any extra money available. She said Uncle Steve had recently engaged an agency to handle the search and after a month received the report.

It stated that Frank at one time had a previous marriage. She was the daughter of a coffee plantation owner down in Brazil. From the information gathered, there was a history of domestic violence and Frank had a drinking and womanizing problem, even back then. He was a prime suspect when they found parts of the father-in-law's body in a grinding machine. The authorities said it was an accident and as soon as they exonerated Frank from all guilt, he left Brazil on a freighter. His trail from then on was difficult to follow. He was jumping so many ships, his whereabouts ended in complete oblivion. Many of her family thought his wife went with him, but from some witnesses questioned, they said Frank was definitely traveling alone. It was a very quiet trip going back home. Chills were running up and down my spine as I thought about the report from the agency and I could tell by the way my ma sat quietly staring out the window, she also was digesting that information. There wasn't any counting of cows this time.

It wasn't easy leaving the excitement of Chicago and going home to our quiet little city, but home is home and I couldn't wait to tell all the things I saw to my neighborhood pals. They always sat with great interest as I related my trips to the big city, where millions of people lived. My fear heading back was that Frank would be there with diabolical plans on how to become a widower again.

Chapter 32

It was after my episode with Wilber and advice from my friend Snort, I started looking for someone closer to my age. I knew if my ma ever found out about Wilber's desires, she would have demanded it. I didn't have to search very long for a new pal...he found me. His name was Robert Stroll. His parents owned the Stroll dairy and ice cream parlor downtown on Franklin Street.

Bobby was in some of my classes at St. Mary's and because he was very overweight for his age, we called him Blubber. That nickname was later cut down to just Blub. He was the only red headed kid I ever knew they didn't call Red. Blub always wanted to be on my side whenever we played games at recess or lunch hour. He was a nice likeable kid, but wasn't very well coordinated and I was reluctant to choose him. The thing he was good at was swimming. He loved skinny-dipping and was constantly doing the pickle on the plate routine. With his fat belly blocking his view, I don't think he could even see his pickle on a plate.

I was biking home from school one day when I heard a voice calling, "Hey, Michael, wait up." When I looked back, I saw Blub laboriously running to catch up with me.

"Hey Blub, how come you're walking?" His mother always drove him to and from school. Struggling to catch his breath he said, "Do you mind if I talk to you a minute, Michael?"

"What happened, Blub, did your mother forget to pick you up?"

"No, I told her I wanted to walk, because I knew you always took this way home and I wanted to ask you something, okay?"

"Ya, I don't mind Blub...what's up?" In fact, I didn't mind associating with a kid considered high society. Mr. Stroll besides owning the dairy was also a high-ranking officer in the Indiana National Guard. "I am going to visit my dad at the National Guard camp at Indianapolis and he said I could invite a friend to come with me, how about it Michael?" I had mixed emotions because of a terrible accident that happened on a Halloween night. A group of 'older guys' dreamed up an idea to play pranks on local residents. It wasn't supposed to cause property damage. How I got included with the adventure is still a puzzle. There were five guys including me. The prank was; the group sneaks up to a house at night with sacks full of collected garbage and tin cans filled with water. One of the houses we sneaked up on was my pal, Blub. When we reached the house, we planned to throw the garbage over the porch railing. The racket was supposed to scare the occupants inside and give them a lot of cleaning up to do in the morning. As it happened, the front of the house had a large beautiful multi-colored bay window. The whole windowpane had artistically designed squares. At the whispered signal, let's go, we dashed to the porch. My heart went up in my throat when I heard the terrible sound of glass shattering. Someone in our group became overzealous and flung his contribution too far. It must have contained some water filled tin cans. Needless to say, we high-tailed out of there and went to the safety of our homes. I know I did. When I came in the house, my ma, as always, knew by looking at me, something was wrong. She said," you are as red as a beet and out of breath." I didn't want to lie, so I told her, I just had a race with four other guys. I never heard how much the colorful bay window cost, but the insurance company hired a detective to find the culprits that did the dastardly prank.

The next day I was gone from early morning till late in the evening, at the cities marble championship. When I pulled up on my bike, he was waiting to interrogate me on my exploits the evening before. I told him I didn't know who did it and I wasn't lying. It was dark and with five guys hurling at the same time, it was impossible. I could see it was the end of the day of questioning and he didn't have a clue. I was his last interview and he asked, "Well kid, how do I know you have been at a marble tournament all day?" I looked directly in his eyes and responded with, "Well, maybe this will prove it, Sir." I then handed him my marble champ blue ribbon.

I felt guilty, but jumped at the opportunity to accept Blub's invitation to go with him to the army camp in Indianapolis. My search for a new pal had just ended. He was my age and from a good Catholic family. I knew that would please my ma. The only thing that didn't make the situation perfect, was the fact that now when I'd choose my team, I had to pick him.

"I'll have to ask my ma first, but I don't think there will be any problem Blub."

How right I was. She thought it would be a good experience for me, to see how my heroic father, Lt. Nerveroski once lived as a soldier.

My ma packed me a small suitcase with toiletries, a bathing suit and a change of clothes. I met Blub at the bus terminal downtown and with two round trip tickets from Mr. Stroll; we rode the bus to Indianapolis. There were two soldiers waiting at the station and drove us in a Jeep to an army base outside of town. Upon arriving, I was surprised our cots were right in the officers' barracks.

We spent most of the day playing pool, ping-pong and using the boxing equipment. I was surprised at the punch Blub could deliver. The soldiers were usually gone all day on training maneuvers, which meant we had the recreation hall to ourselves. I felt like someone special eating with the officers at mess. Mr. Stroll sat at the head of table with Blub on the right and me on the left. Other officers occupied the rest of the table. I couldn't tell what rank they each held, but I could see Mr. Stroll was 'Top Gun.' I couldn't wait to tell my ma about the huge amount of food served and all the second helpings I wanted. It was strange to see soldiers working as waiters. They stood at attention waiting to refill water glasses, or in my case, ice-cold lemonade. To top it all off they were even calling me Sir.

After a few days of having the run of the recreation hall, we became bored with the equipment and thought it would be fun for a change to go to the city's public swimming pool downtown. Major Stroll gave his permission, but reminded us to act like good soldiers. He ordered a driver to take us to the pool and gave us extra spending money. He said our driver would come back to pick us up in two hours.

Indianapolis at that time had been suffering from a long heat wave. It was a good thing that the pool was quite large, because there were many swimmers using it. We paid our fee and entered the fenced area that surrounded the pool. There was a high diving board at one end, where the depth was twelve feet. It tapered down to only three feet on the other end, where steps led down into the water. We quickly removed our clothing down to our bathing suits and neatly stacked our clothes by the fence. It didn't take long for us to meet and make friends with a couple of local boys our age. What seemed strange about them was, Indianapolis is only a hundred and some miles from our hometown, yet they spoke with a heavy southern drawl. We teased them by mimicking the way they talked. They in turn mimicked the way we sounded to them. I pulled Blub aside and said, "Let's show them our pickle on a plate routine."

"What if the lifeguard sees us and kicks us out of the pool, Michael?"

"Well, maybe if we go to the shallow end and do it quickly, he won't notice." We asked our two friends if they would like to see what we do at our swimming hole up north. They said, "Ya we'd like to see what ya'all do up thar' and mabbe we could start doing it down here." We went to the shallow end of the pool, where there were only a few little kids splashing around. We positioned our friends so they could block the lifeguard's view as he playfully teased some foxy girls. When we were ready, I turned and said, "Now Blub!" We quickly pulled down our trunks, floated on our backs and shouted, "Pickle on a plate...pickle on a plate."

This started our two friends laughing and splashing water at our pickles. It all stopped being funny when my eyes cleared from the splashing and I looked up to see a lifeguard staring down at me. He had one hand on his hip and the other hand signaling with his thumb to get out of the pool. I had no idea where he came from, but we learned later that there wasn't one, but two guards on duty. He grabbed us by the ear, took us to our clothes and led us out to the gate. We tried to appease him by stating we were future soldiers from up north and here on vacation. It didn't make an impression on him, because he opened the gate, gave each of our dupa's a hard boot and said, "GO BACK TO YOUR HICK TOWN AND TAKE YOUR

LITTLE PICKLES WITH YOU!" He must have thought his statement was hilarious, because he couldn't wait to relate it to the giggling beauties.

Major Stroll asked if we enjoyed ourselves and we told him, ya, we got a...big KICK out of it. (No pun intended!) I wish I could have stayed a few more days, but it was Saturday and I had to go back to see my first big league baseball game in Chicago on Sunday. I also had great concern about being gone so long and my ma alone with Frank.

Chapter 33

E ach year at the end of the baseball season Stash treated his team with a trip to Chicago to see a White Sox game at Cominskey Park. He borrowed a truck from one his suppliers, loaded his players in the back and had a keg of iced-down beer for the trip. They were all pretty well on their way to getting snockered by the time they reached the stadium. Everyone except me and the designated driver, Stash. We had them back in my day too.

I only helped a few times as the batboy, so I was surprised when Stash asked me if I wanted to come along. I told him I would have to ask my ma first, because the trip was on a Sunday and I would be missing Mass. She said we could go to church on Saturday night and if I promised to ride up in front of the truck, I could go. I think she knew the players would be drinking and she didn't want me back there with all the swearing and sexual boasting going on. I could have won any bicycle race with the speed I attained going back to tell Stash the good news.

The starting time for the double-header was one o'clock in the afternoon, so we had to leave the tavern early Sunday morning. When Stash informed us the visiting team was the New York Yankees, I almost fainted from the excitement. Wow I thought, the New York Yankees with Mickey Mantle, Yogi Berra and the rest of their powerful line-up. The whole day was such an exciting experience that my heart didn't calm down until I finally fell asleep on the way home. I couldn't wait to tell my ma about the home run Al Simmons hit in each game to sweep the double-header from the Yankees.

When we arrived back at the tavern, it was well after eight o'clock in the evening and because it was in the fall of the year, it had already turned dark. While Stash and I carried the empty kegs back into the storeroom, he kept calling up the stairs to let Hilda know he was home. When she didn't respond, he went upstairs to see why. A few minutes later, he came hurrying down with a puzzled look on his face. He quickly grabbed a flashlight and headed out the back door toward the garage. I was running right behind him wondering why he was so concerned. I asked, "What's the matter Stash? Is there something wrong?" He stood there staring into space and when he finally spoke, the words hit me like a bolt of lightning.

"Hilda has left me and taken the car, he shouted."

"What do you mean she left you? Maybe she didn't know when you'd be home and went to a late movie or something." Knowing Hilda, that something could be taking place somewhere out in the cemetery.

He held up a piece of paper and said, "She left me this note." He quickly crumpled the paper in his massive fist I knew he wasn't going to reveal the message to anyone...not even me. When I left for home, Stash was sitting at the bar with his forehead resting on his arms. I asked if he was going to be all right and without looking up, he waved his hand for me to leave. I knew he didn't want me to see that he was crying. I too shed tears as I biked home. Not for that 'Shoestring' Hilda, but for the terrible pain that was ripping at the heart of my best friend. On the way, I wondered if Frank passed his audition with 'flying colors' that night in the cemetery and Hilda chose him to be the guy she was waiting to run off with. This was the one and only time I wanted Frank to be home when I got there.

Although it was well past my ma's bedtime, she was waiting up for me. She was the typical mother that worries until all her children are back home safe in their beds. She said she heard the games on the radio and wanted to hear all about the trip. I knew I couldn't do that until I asked her the only thing that was important at the time. "Ma, have you seen Frank lately?" I held my breath waiting for her answer.

"No, he hasn't been home all weekend, Januscheck; he must be staying out on the docks." It was then I knew I had to reveal to someone what I saw in the cemetery, but to whom? I couldn't tell my ma, not Stash, not Aunt Helen or anybody for that matter. There was still an outside chance I was wrong about the identity of the two people on the blanket. After all, it was late at night and I was tired and sleepy-eyed. I kept telling myself this, but in the back of my mind I was quite convinced that the two adulterers I saw in the glow of the lighter, was my stepfather Frank and Stash's wife...Hilda.

Chapter 34

Going to school the next day, I noticed a police car parked in front of Stash's Tavern. I wanted to stop and find out the reason they were there, but I had overslept and didn't want a tardy mark on my report card. I planned to check it out on my way home. The clock on the wall took forever to reach three in the afternoon. When the school bell finally rang, I grabbed my books, made a mad dash out the doors and headed straight for the tavern. Upon my arrival, I could see a few more police cars, plus a van with the words CRIME LAB written on the side. I wondered if they considered running away from your husband a felony. They had locked the tavern door with a big sign on the front that read: CLOSED. I remembered you could get to the back through a space between the tavern and the building next door; the same opening Snowflake and Curly must have gone through on their fatal trip to my house. The space was very narrow, but I was thin enough to squeeze through sideways. I knew if Stash was there, I'd be able to stay and find out what was going on. It was a lucky thing he saw me first and told the cops that I was one of his employees that was with him last night. What seemed strange, the detectives gathered around Snowflake and Curly's tombstone, which now was turned perpendicular on its base. I noticed it swung around on an iron rod that came up from the stone foundation. When it turned like that, it revealed a hidden compartment in the base. Stash said there was enough room for two large moneybags. He didn't think Hilda could have taken the money, because the headstone weighed over two hundred pounds. The detective believed there could have been someone helping her. I wanted to say; ya...like some drunken sailor, but thought better of it at the time and would save my opinion for a later date.

Stash's tombstone idea for hiding money was only good if no one saw him putting his savings in there. He said he always hid his money at three or four in the morning when everyone was asleep. There wasn't any need for a flashlight, because he could do it in the dark. Stash must not have thought about the nights when the moon was full and their bedroom window afforded a direct view down at the tombstone. Maybe there was a moonlit night when Hilda awoke and saw him stuffing the money in that canine crypt.

It certainly answered the question of how he got such a glamorous girl like Hilda. What better way to find the hiding place for the Wolinski treasure, than to marry into the family. She was now a very rich woman on her way with one of her auditioned partners. God only knows where.

Chapter 35

When Frank didn't show up at the house for three weekends in a row, I had to convince my ma and even me for that matter, he was gone forever. I told her I was going to give a final check to see if he has been staying out on the docks. It was nearing the end of the warm fishing months and the crews were working double shifts to beat the ice that would soon be forming. There was still an outside chance that at the end of the day, Frank was so exhausted he was staying on the tug to rest for the early morning run. My ma wasn't too concerned because Frank would stay away for many weeks at a time and then suddenly show up without giving any reason for his absence. She also learned never to question his whereabouts or activities unless she was ready for one of his tyrannical outbursts, which usually ended with him hitting her. The blows were so severe she walked around with a sprained neck for weeks. I could always tell if Frank had been home by the bruises on her body. I asked her many times why she never reported the beatings to the police. She said a wife should understand her husband and try not to bring any shame upon him. She always blamed herself for getting him so agitated. When I told Aunt Helen what she said, her explanation was, back in Poland, the man was king of the household and his actions never questioned. I'm sure that's not true today.

I waited until the following Saturday to bike out to the docks. Frank still hadn't come home and although I was sure, he was somewhere satisfying Hilda, I had to prove my theory. Arriving at the docks, I went directly to the area where they moored the tugs. My scenario of Frank and Hilda running off with Stash's moneybags was proving to be a real possibility. Frank hadn't been out to the docks for quite a while and his crew was pissed off at him for not showing up. I wanted to say, with all the money Frank had stolen, he probably owns his own boat, not an old tugger but a beautiful yacht.

I begged my ma to tell the authorities about his absence, but because of her old beliefs, she just kept it to herself. When I asked Aunt Helen, her final advice to the whole situation was, everyone is better off without him. Leave it that way!

Chapter 36

Stash was getting calls every day from police stations coast to coast giving him descriptions of women they had in custody and I am sure he still had hopes that Hilda would be coming back. Knowing Stash, he would have forgiven her and offered to start life all over again in any big city of her choice, which was Chicago.

After waiting several days for information on Hilda, a call came in from a small town in West Texas. The authorities found a woman murdered in a motel room on the outskirts of the city. Stash's description of Hilda on the F.B.I. missing list, was a woman in her late twenties, five foot six, blue eyes and blond hair. They said the woman they found fit those features, but they wanted more information like dental records, tattoos, scars or any birthmarks. He had informed them that as far as he knew, Hilda never needed a dentist, because her teeth were so perfect. Her body had absolutely no blemishes or markings for identification. He said he could prove that it was Hilda if they would look for a certain birthmark hidden from view and told them exactly where to find it. The newspaper article stated within minutes the call came back from Texas. They found the birthmark and were certain the body was Stash's Hilda.

One of the 'older guys' at the pow-wow informed us where that mark on her body was discovered. He said his old man was a cop on the force and he overheard him tell his drunken 'buddies' at a Friday night poker party, it was a little mole at the tip of her vagina, just inside the folds of her labia. To give the story some class, that's my description. He described it as...a freckle in the crack of her snatch. That was typical at every pow-wow, short on words and to the point.

The information stated they found Hilda lying nude face down on a bed with her hands and legs tied in a spread-eagle position. She had been brutally beaten, strangled with a telephone cord and sodomized while in that position. The only clue they had was the bindings were tied with sailor knots. When Stash asked them if there was any money found, the answer was...not one red cent.

The police believed the case would be difficult to solve, because the clerk at the motel said the blond woman was the one that registered for the room. They had no knowledge or description of anyone else with her.

The F.B.I in its infant stages was only handling federal cases. It was up to the city authorities to pursue the case and with only the clue of the sailor knots to go on, the police department in this small town finally stored it away in their files as unsolved.

"Ma, there is no doubt in my mind that it is Frank."

She shook her finger at me and said, "Januscheck, this is a port city and I am sure there were a lot of sailors that patronized Stash's tavern, so it's not good to blame Frank just because of the sailor knot."

Oh my dear Mother, if she only knew what I knew about Frank and Hilda in the cemetery that night, but I just couldn't divulge my secret of using the telescope to watch people having sex. I knew Frank was prone to beating women, but could he go as far as killing one? They say that after the first, to murder the second time becomes a lot easier and they never discovered what happened to Frank's Brazilian wife. Little did I know at my innocent age, the lengths men would go for money. Tragedies of that kind were very rare in my peaceful town. It reminded me of a line from a mystery program on the radio back then...Who knows what evil lurks in the hearts of men...'only the shadow knows.'

In fact, up until Hilda was murdered, there had been only one other local killing. I heard about it at a sandlot pow-wow, of course. Here are the details of the crime:

It was about a young wife who was a big fan of the movie star Rudolph Valentino. She wouldn't miss any of his movies and always stayed for a double feature. She cherished an eight by ten glossy personally autographed to her. The story goes; she displayed the picture on the mantle in her living room. When her husband hinted that he wanted sex that night, she would secretly hide the picture under her pillow. While the husband was huffing and puffing away, she would hold the picture of the movie star behind his head. She was evidently pretending it was her heartthrob of the silver screen. I don't know how many times or how long she had been getting away with it, but when she did get caught, it cost her life. The husband beat her to death with the heavy metal picture frame. At his trial, he pleaded not guilty because of temporary insanity. He said he went out of his mind when he caught his wife in bed having sex with Rudolph Valentino!

In case you'd like to know, Rudolph Valentino died at an early age from bleeding ulcers. For decades after that, women were still bringing roses to place on his grave.

Chapter 37

Wen informed by the authorities that they indeed had the body with the specified beauty mark, Stash headed for Texas. Customers immediately started asking questions as to what funeral home she would be at and what plot in Greenwood Cemetery her body would lay.

When Stash finally returned, he surprised everyone by stating he had already laid Hilda to rest. That was all he would say on the subject and he said it with such finality in his voice, no one dared pursue it any further.

After the devastating loss of his wife, Stash became a completely different person. The spirit of life which once abounded in his heart, died along with his Hilda. He lost all interest in the activities at the bar and I knew the inevitable would soon be happening. Stash informed everyone he was turning the tavern over to another member of the Wolinski clan and had special leasing conditions. The tavern and property was not to change in any way. There was to be no remodeling and as things wore out, they had to repair or replace them to keep the same motif.

These stipulations proved to be a big factor in keeping the tavern one of the most popular places in Northern Indiana. While the other bars were always modernizing through the years, Stash's stayed the same and thus it became one of the unique places to see. Today when a customer takes his first step into the bar, he gets a magical feeling of being back into the notorious years of the gay nineties. The furnishings are all antique, including the multi-colored chipped glass shades on the lights that hang from the ceiling. The long mahogany bar and stools date back to the prohibition era. The typical old player piano with all the fancy carved scrollwork plays songs of the past for all to sing and it still only costs a dime. Today they call it Karaoke. The only changes are from updating the health codes to stainless steel equipment, most of which is behind the bar or back in the kitchen. They placed the old brass spittoons around the room, but now they display bouquets of colorful waxed flowers. The metal trough that ran along the bottom of the bar no longer has running water. There was a time when customers could spit their tobacco juice right down into the trough and the water would flush the ugly brown saliva away. Not only did they spit into that trough, but one guy got kicked out for using it as a urinal. He evidently couldn't leave his drink long enough to go to the can. Stash caught him with his dick hanging down, pissing into the trough and at the same time gulping down a foaming mug of beer. It gave credence to the old adage...going in one end and coming out the other.

It was on a Sunday when the bar was closed, that Stash hired me to help him get things ready for the new owner. There was a lot to be done, so we started early in the morning. When I entered the bar, I was shocked to see Stash sitting at a table that had a bottle of scotch on it. I couldn't believe my eyes, because he never touched the stuff before. I was hoping someone left it on the table from the previous night. Those hopes were soon shattered when I saw him lift it to his mouth and take a big swallow. I wondered at the time if he was using booze to help cope with the loss of his Hilda. If drinking was helping him face reality, I could only hope time would soon cure his wounds. I feared that Stash would become mean from drinking the way Frank always did. Although he nipped at the bottle all day, his mild disposition never changed.

When we completed our work, Stash took the half-empty bottle of Scotch, staggered over to a table and motioned with his hand for me to join him. I could see by his blood-shot eyes that the booze was affecting him. He was having a difficult time trying to keep them open. With a slight slur of his words he said, "Sid down Michael. Do ya wanna know bout Hilda?" His question was quite a surprise to me. I couldn't believe he would give me that information.

"Gee Stash; you don't have to explain it to me. It doesn't really matter," I assured him.

"Well I gotta tell somebody Michael. I'd like to know if my judgment of what I did with her remains would be considered okay." I couldn't believe what I was hearing. Why was he telling me, instead of someone in his family? I realized then what a great friendship and respect we had for each other. I also realized he would make a terrific father.

He proceeded to tell me he drove down to Texas, with the intention of sending Hilda's body back by rail in a white casket, then placing her in a funeral home until laid to rest in Greenwood Cemetery. He said the more he thought about it, the more his plans changed. He believed Hilda wouldn't want to be on display for all to gawk at, especially the women who envied her beauty. So instead he had her body cremated and all the religious rites performed in Texas.

He said, "I planned on placing the urn containing her ashes on the dresser in our bedroom, but got the feeling it wouldn't be where Hilda really wanted to end up. She always said she'd like to be in a big exciting city like Chicago, so that's where I headed. When I got there,

I hired a taxi and told the cabbie to drive downtown through the Loop. I told him I planned to scatter my wife's ashes out the window. I gave him a twenty-dollar bill and asked if it would be all right. He said, "Buddy, for twenty bucks I'd scatter them myself." So little by little, I emptied Hilda's ashes on the streets of that great Metropolis. The way the winds blow and swirl around that windy city, remains of Hilda could now be trapped in nooks and crannies all over the streets and buildings of that big shopping center."

When it looked like Stash had passed out; the sudden rise of his head and the slamming of his massive fist on the table startled me.

"I'm gonna find that son-of-a-bitch, Michael. I don't know how or where, but I'll get him." The force of the blow shook the table so hard it raised it off its legs, causing the bottle to tip over and I had to catch it before it crashed to the floor.

"He's not gonna get away with what he did to my Hilda."

"But Stash, how could you search for someone that you don't have a description of or even begin to guess his whereabouts?"

His demeanor calmed a little as he started telling me his plans. "Well, because of those knots, Michael, it must have been a sailor. They were evidently heading for Mexico or the West coast. There is a good chance he could be around the docks in San Diego."

I was surprised how Stash had suddenly changed from an intoxicated wimp, into an avenging warrior. He said he would start by asking the locals on the docks about any newcomer trying to impress them with his riches. He said, "I know it's like looking for a needle in a haystack, Michael, but maybe I'll get lucky." The way Lady Luck was treating him; it didn't look like the odds were in his favor. He didn't really have much to go on, but knowing Stash, I was sure he would search the ends of the earth to destroy the person who murdered his beautiful wife. I just couldn't stand by and let my friend waste all the years it would probably take to find the culprit. I had an idea that would aid in his search. I said, "Stash, I am going to give you a lead to the guy I think you are looking for. I've kept it a secret for a long time and I know you won't divulge it to anyone else." I didn't want to add any more facts about Hilda's sexual exploits to this already heartbroken man, but felt it had to be done.

I said, "Stash if you let me, I could help you with your search."

"How would you do that Michael? You know you can't come with me."

"Yes, I know, but I am positive the sailor you are looking for is my step-father, Frank." Although it was difficult for me to get the words out, I proceeded to relate to him about Frank and Hilda in the cemetery. I told him how I was using a telescope to watch people having sex there on Saturday nights.

"I've kept it a secret from my ma, because she would have restricted me from playing with the telescope. We haven't seen Frank since the night of the robbery and neither has his crew out at the docks where he works," I added.

"There's a photo of Frank wearing a sailor's cap in a desk drawer at my house. You can use it to show people when you are asking for information. I think it would really help...do you want it?"

"I certainly do, Michael, but I'm not sure I'll be coming back. If I don't, I'll mail it to you. I'm sorry your family got mixed up in this."

"That's okay, Stash. As far as I'm concerned, we didn't consider him part of our family anyhow. You can tear the darn picture up and feed it to the fish for all I care. I'll go home and get the picture and be right back."

When I returned, Stash was sound asleep with his head pillowed by his outstretched arm. In his hand, he held the bottle that was now completely empty of its contents. I gently removed it and in its place, I inserted the picture of a dangerously unscrupulous sailor named...Frank Dramski.

Chapter 38

It seemed my love for storytelling was again manifesting itself. I couldn't get the idea out of my head that here was a great one waiting for someone to tell. The hero would be Stash and the exploits of the Wolinski family. They could even make it into a hit movie. I realized I didn't know anything about writing a movie script, but there are screenwriters to handle that job. All they needed was the complete story. Well anyway, that is what they told me. I planned to call the movie 'Stash's'. You could shoot many of the scenes at the tavern itself. The cast would have to include the adolescent Polish boy with his telescope. The part about him putting his peepka between his legs would have to be left out and describing in detail the events taking place at the orgies. I wouldn't even bring up the older guys and all their crude sexual experiences offered at the pow-wows. Instead, I would have the boy strictly using the telescope while playing soldier from his bedroom window. It would be by accident that one night he sees Stash's wife Hilda and his stepfather Frank embracing. Kissing would be as far as you could go and absolutely no nudity. The audiences in my day had to assume the rest.

It's hard to believe how strict the movie censors were about the dialogue. An actor couldn't even say the word shit, although he stepped in a pile of it. Open mouth kissing was not allowed or a peck held longer than a few seconds. The only way the director could show how the hero had the 'hots' for the female star, was the sudden smashing of his mouth on hers. I often wondered if the scene had several retakes, would she end up with lips like a Ubangi. They did not allow the strong language back then either. For instance, the last scene in Gone with the Wind, Rhett Butler, played by Clark Gable, is standing at the front door leaving Scarlet O'Hara, played by Vivian Leigh. She is pleading with him not to leave. "Where will I go, what will I do, Rhett?"

Clark's famous line that completely shocked the packed theaters throughout the country went something like this... "Frankly my dear... I really don't give a damn." When he said the word damn, you could hear a loud gasp from the audience and the women were so shocked they were near fainting and had to fan themselves with their dainty white handkerchiefs. It was the first time they wrote a word as strong as damn for a line in a movie. Today's screenwriters however would probably write that scene like this: Scarlet would ask..."Where will I go, what will I do, Rhett?" Clark would turn and give that eye squinting, mouth-puckering smile of his and say... "Frankly my dear... I really don't give a rats ass." (I wanted to use a word that rhymes with duck but just couldn't do it.)

As a youth, I really didn't care for epic movies. My favorites were western sagas... where men are men and smelled like horses. Cowboy toughness was rated on how far he could spit his chewing tobacco. I also wondered in the barroom brawls, how the ten-gallon hat of the hero never came off. I can't remember John Wayne passionately kissing any hot cowgirl. For a young boy, ughhhh!

I had dreamed up many nerve-racking situations that Stash could have run into in his search for Frank. I also thought of an exciting and surprising ending. The way things turned out, my idea for the ending was so close to what actually happened, you would think I had a crystal ball of my own.

Every few days Stash was making calls to the tavern reporting his location and activities. After a few weeks, those messages suddenly stopped and there was great concern for his safety. About a month later, an article appeared in the local newspaper. It stated the F.B.I. had visited our Coast Guard Station looking for information on sailors past and present. The report went on to say that a pleasure boat exploded and burned a mile out from a San Diego marina. The blast was so powerful that only splinters of the boat floated among the debris. Authorities believed insatiable feeding sharks cleaned up all human flesh. The reason their investigation brought them all the way to our harbor was a picture of a sailor found on what was left of the charred wreckage. It was a headshot of a man wearing a sailor cap and on the back; it had the name and address of the photographer. Although they did not show the picture, I had a good idea who it was and where the picture was taken.

Every summer one of our city's photography studios had a booth on the midway in the Washington Park amusement area. They would offer special deals for vacationers wanting souvenirs of their trip. It being a port city, most customers wanted to have their picture taken wearing a sailor cap supplied by the studio. The photo of Frank that I gave Stash came from there.

After 'putting two and two together,' I had a sickening revelation that hit me in the pit of my stomach. That picture they found meant one of the fatalities had to be my dearest friend Stash. I could only hope Frank must have perished with him. The name and address of the photographer on the back of the picture, led the investigation by the F.B.I. to our Coast Guard Station.

I supposed you are wondering if in the last scene I would have the hero Stash killed along with the villain Frank. Well, at the time, I was in a great quandary whether I should go with fiction or truth. With fiction, I could save Stash, but the truth would be more shocking. I was never able to pursue my story any further, because of devastating events in my life, that were waiting to happen just around the corner.

Chapter 39

For my birthday, Aunt Helen and Uncle Steve invited us to visit them at their beautiful new home in Chicago. We planned on spending one day shopping in the downtown loop and two days at the Chicago 1933 World's Fair. We met at the station and they took us to their house north of town in a brand new 1933 Packard. I asked, "Is Uncle Steve a millionaire ma?"

"I don't think he's that rich yet, but he's head of the bookkeeping department. It's a very large international business and if his investments in the company pay off, he could become very rich." His work didn't leave him much free time, however, so just the three of us went shopping and visited the fair.

The downtown loop with its tall skyscrapers was awesome to me. I wondered if some of those structures could have bits of Hilda's ashes in the corners of the windows, even as high up as the top floors. For that matter, we could even be stepping on her ashes. Maybe my ma and Aunt Helen were, but I never stepped on a crack. I was the only one that knew about Hilda's ashes and the eerie feeling that her spirit was everywhere gave me the creeps. I couldn't wait until we left for the fair.

We spent two whole days at the fair and still didn't have time to see all the big attractions and movie stars. One of which was the famous fan-dancer Sally Rand. My ma hurried me past the entrance of the building because of a life- sized cardboard statue out in front, with feathered fans barely covering her naked body. The attraction I was most amazed at was an African tribe performing great feats for the fair audiences. It was the only time other than Mr. Washington I ever saw a black person. The tribesmen with their long spears performed naked, except for a cloth that barely covered their peepka area. I asked my ma why they weren't wearing a fig leaf like Adam and Eve. She said, "What they're wearing Januscheck is called a loincloth."

Aunt Helen interrupted with, "Ya, fig leafs don't cover enough." The two women burst out in uncontrollable laughter, but I couldn't understand the humor in her statement. I found myself wishing Snort had made the trip with us.

With faces streaked of white paint and a necklace strung with large animal fangs, they started chanting and dancing barefoot over beds of red-hot coals. What astounded me were their faces never showed any sign of pain and they didn't stop dancing until the coals had turned to ashes. My ma told me that the bottoms of their feet were tough from going barefoot in the jungle. I said, "Heck ma, I always go barefoot in the summer, but it didn't help me one bit down that yellow brick road." Maybe I should have danced the way they're doing instead of skipping like Huck Finn.

I told my ma I wished grandfather had picked Chicago instead of our little town. She then explained to me how our port city came close to being the biggest city in the Midwest, instead of Chicago. She said that at one time there was a great need to expand a harbor, large enough to handle the amount of grain and farm produce, along with lumber and fish. When the big railroad companies were planning to build routes to either the Chicago port or ours, there was under-handed trickery taking place. Although at that time Chicago and our city were about the same in size, our Trail Creek was more favorable for harbor use than the Chicago Rivers. The Chicago executives schemed to minimize the use of our city for shipping, by listing themselves as the leading port, even for cargo shipped aboard vessels from our harbor. Then they took credit for loading lumber, flour and other products even if Chicago had none to ship. When it came time to decide who was shipping the most, the railroads of course chose Chicago. "So you see, Januscheck, that wonderful western metropolis grew elsewhere and not at the foot of our famous sand dune, 'The Hoosier Slide.'

I was surprised that my ma knew so much about the history of our city. I asked her if she had ever seen the dune called, 'The Hoosier Slide. "No, Januscheck, it was long gone before your grandfather came here from Poland. For many years, the towering sand dune stood west of the Trail Creek entrance, right at the spot where the Northern Indiana Public Service station now stands. We see that big building across the harbor when we are fishing on the pier. That sand dune stood one hundred and seventy-five feet high, at its peak. Tourists from all over the world came to see nature's awesome structure. People climbed to its top to have picnics, take panoramic pictures and even hold weddings. There were contests to see who could climb the highest, bare-footed, without stopping. Professional football players out of Chicago came to strengthen their legs by sand giving way under their footing, as they ran up the steep slope." There were two N.F.L. teams; the Bears and the Cardinals.

"Gee, ma, I wish it was still there so I could strengthen my legs for pitching. What ever happened to it?"

"Well, from what I've been told, Januscheck, the men used the trees for erecting buildings in town. Then with the dune lacking trees, wind would blow sand into the city and cause dessert-like sand storms."

"Well then, where did it all go, ma?"

"You'll be surprised to know that a lot of it was sold to build Chicago. Even the jars I use in canning are made from that sand. They used it to make plate-glass for companies in Muncie and Kokomo, Indiana and industries all over the United States. They built most of the bathing beaches on our inland lakes with sand from that enormous dune. So you see, Januscheck, there is a bit of 'Hoosier Slide' from coast to coast, Canada to Mexico and well beyond. Our town wasn't as big as Chicago but like the fat lady, we saw at the World's Fair, we cover a lot more ground. If it makes you feel any better, your grandfather wanted you to grow up in a quieter environment."

We were so tired from all the non-stop activity in Chicago, my ma and I fell asleep on the way home. It was a good thing that the conductor was standing right by our seat when he yelled, "Next stop M...oops, I almost gave the name of the town, again. His booming voice woke us up in time to gather our souvenirs and head for the exit. There is certainly a lot of truth in the song, "Be it ever so humble, there's no place like home," except if Frank was there.

It was nice to be back in my old neighborhood and among my playmates again. I know my ma was anxious to get back to the paper hanging jobs she had on her schedule. A few days later she asked, "Have you seen or noticed anything different around the place, Michael? It seems like something is missing, but I can't put my finger on it. Maybe you might know what it is?"

"For one thing, ma, I haven't heard any voices or sounds coming from the renters next door."

"You're right, now that you mention it; I haven't seen Mr. Melon or Mr. Balan since we came back from Chicago." The men were always having some kind of drunken argument and at times, their shouting got so loud we could hear them through the non-insulated wall that separated our two buildings. There were times we knew the arguments had turned into fistfights by the sounds of bodies bumping against the wall. So hard at times, it rattled the dishes in our dining room china closet. It's a wonder they didn't kill each other.

Mr. Melon and Mr. Balan were the only names I knew them by and I seldom got a good look at them. There was a padded porch swing available, but for some reason they never spent any leisure time outside. My ma said they were from the state of Mississippi. They were tall and thin as a rail. You could tell by their attire they came from areas of wide-open ranges or plantations. They wore Stetson hats, western boots and belts with large buckles. Their jeans fit so tight; I wondered how they could bend down to pick anything up. Both were extremely bow-legged, which led me to believe that when they were kids, they had bad eating habits, or maybe they rode too many fat horses. We waited a few days for any sign of them and when they didn't show, we decided to check out the unit.

After searching through the rooms, there were definite indications they left in a hurry, leaving army boots, a confederate soldiers Kepi cap, like the one worn by Mr. Washington and above all, their treasured Southern Flag. It was still hanging on the wall above the bed. They also forfeited the rent money they had coming back. My ma's lease stated that if the renter moved out before the full month was up, they could get back a pro-rated amount. They apparently never used one room, which was the second bedroom. It didn't occur to me until my later years that Mr. Melon and Mr. Balan were bunking together. I guess that's the reason they fought like a married couple. After a week, it became apparent they weren't coming back, so we started getting the unit ready for new renters.

It would usually take a full week to get the place back in shape again. We had to go over every inch, making sure it was spotlessly clean. Something always needed painting and if there was any crayon or pencil marks on the walls, my ma had to re-paper the whole room. In Mr. Melon and Mr. Balan's case, it was replacing the broken dishes. In spite of the loss of rent money, my ma said she was happy that the duplex was empty and maybe now Mr. Washington could move in. I knew she was thinking about adjusting his leasing conditions until later. I wondered how she could still think of him. We hadn't seen Mr. Washington going past our house for a year of Sundays, which was strange.

Yes, that was typical of my ma.

Chapter 40

I became quite concerned when my ma asked me if I would shine up grandfather's war memorabilia. She said she was thinking of giving them to the church to raise money at one of their auctions. Hearing there was a possibility that the helmet and telescope could soon be gone, was like a blow to my solar plexus. Not able to play soldier again or what was even worse, watch the lovers fornicating on Saturday nights, would be a devastating loss. I said, "Ma those are grandfather's prize collections. You aren't going to give those things away, are you?"

"I know they are, Januscheck, but what good are they doing gathering dust upstairs in the closet? I'm sure the church will find some good use for the money." Oh, how I wanted to say, "Hey ma, I'm finding a very good use for them by getting a heck of a sex education." Naturally, I held back that information.

What I did suggest was that grandfather purposely wanted the articles for us to remember him. I didn't know if my psychological ploy would change her mind, so I made sure I didn't miss using the telescope a single Saturday night after that. As I grew older, I found myself beginning to pay more attention to the role some girls were playing in the sex act. I believed that girls only did it, because their boyfriend wanted it. It was quite a shock the first time I saw a girl getting on top and continuing the action. The excitement of watching the girl willingly performing the dominant role, made the aching in my groin become stronger than ever. I would try to fight the urge to stick my peepka between my thighs, but would finally give in to the pressure.

One night while watching the heated action, I started to arrange my peepka and to my surprise, it wasn't limp...but stiff. It was pushing out the material of my pants forming a bulge. When I tried shoving it between my thighs, it wouldn't stay and kept popping back out. I panicked at the frightening thought that from now on, when I viewed the Saturday night episodes, I couldn't use my technique for easing the pressure. It was very disheartening, because in my situation at home, a stiff peepka was as useful as a tit on a boar. From then on, the "boner" as the older guys called it would develop whenever I got the ache in my groin and that too was happening more frequently than before.

Chapter 41

The excitement of changing schools from St. Mary's to the big public high school, kept me from thinking about anything else. It dawned on me one day that my ma would have to register me as having a mother and father. Frank had vanished for years and there was still the possibility my theory of Frank being Hilda's partner in the robbery, could be wrong. The fear that he could show up and claim his husband status hung over me like a guillotine.

Things around the property were deteriorating so badly that my ma had to find a handyman who would take fruit and vegetables for his labor. It seemed she found him when a man showed up one day to see what work she wanted done. She said his name was Marvin Boyanski. I liked the name Marvin because it sounded so manly. She said he had been painting the mayor's house on the outside, while she worked on the inside wallpapering the rooms. She said they ate their lunches together and talked about their plans for the future. He worked at the Indiana State Prison a few days a week as a substitute barber and had been taking odd jobs to save money for a shop of his own. He said because of the severe depression, he didn't think his chances were very promising.

At one of their luncheons, my ma said she offered her trade-out idea to Marvin and he took it. His work was well worth the many jars of canned fruit and vegetables she gave him and as it turned out, he was very adept at any job.

Although Marvin was in his mid-forties, he was still a bachelor, which seemed strange to me. He wasn't a bad looking man, but not a Clark Gable either. I guess you would call him just a plain Joe. What I liked about him were his deep-set eyes that just exuded kindness and a smile that had friendly written all over it. His body was starting to show his forty-some-odd years around the waist and except for the graying temples, his face still looked young and void of any aging. I asked him if I could help and maybe learn to be a handyman myself. Marvin was more than willing to teach me and always called me Michael, not Januscheck. I was learning to like him very much; in fact, I started thinking...who knows...maybe he could be my next father. With that possibility in mind, I biked out to the mayor's house to see if I could watch them. I thought it would be a good way to get to know Marvin better.

When I arrived, I was astounded at the size of this large mansion. I couldn't guess at the square footage, but it looked twice the size of our home and duplex combined. I had never been inside such an enormous house before.

I could not believe the dangerous job my ma was doing. My little five-foot mother was tackling rooms that had ceilings ten-feet high. Back in the twenties and thirties, they even papered the ceilings and a border-strip four inches wide circled the room where the ceiling and walls met.

I stood in dreaded fear as I watched her climb high up on the six-foot ladder with the pasted wallpaper folded over on her left hand. She carried it like a waiter with his tray. To free her right hand she had to put the wallpaper brush in her mouth. She would spread the paper onto the ceiling, while walking along on a plank that was only eighteen inches wide. I was amazed at the steady pace she kept as she attached the paper. Not once did she look down at her feet on that narrow plank, for fear of the paper getting off line. When she was finished, the seams were perfectly straight and undetectable. After watching her doing such dangerous work, I planned to become a great major league pitcher and make a lot of money, so she wouldn't have to work like that anymore.

I bet you are wondering if that Gypsy seer let out a big loud guffaw at that plan too.

Chapter 42

Long after the renovation job on the mansion was finished, Marvin was still doing handyman work for us. It was a pleasant surprise when she informed me one day that he would be staying for supper. The invitations started out at once a week, then blossomed into twice a week. He also started going with us on weekend picnics, fishing out on the pier and Sunday trips to the Washington Park Zoo.

It was at one of these outings in Washington Park's Amusement area that I discovered the awesome strength Marvin possessed. The Midway featured a Roller Coaster, Merry-Go-Round, Ferris wheel and a ride called the Whip. It spun around so fast the centrifugal force slid everyone screaming at the top of their voices to one side of the seat. I remembered how dizzy I felt staggering back down the ramp.

Marvin and I went into the Penny Arcade building, where the machines only took a penny to play. The most popular machine for men was the one that measured your grip pressure. He pulled me over, put a penny in the machine and said, "Let's see what you got,

Michael." I put my hand around the handle, squeezed with all my might, but the needle never moved. I even tried both hands at the same time and I still couldn't budge it. "I don't think this is meant for kids my age, Marvin, you try it," I dared him.

He put his hand around the handle and squeezed. To my amazement, the needle went all the way over and a bell rang indicating he reached the top number. He didn't stop at that demonstration, but inserted another penny and accomplished the same thing with his left hand. It was then I noticed how large his wrists were. When I asked him the reason for the strength in his grip, he said it was from many years of squeezing his clippers giving haircuts. He said when one hand got a cramp in it; he would have to switch to the other... thus the power in either hand. Electrical clippers were not on the market back then. It was a relief to know that if Frank ever came back, my ma would have Marvin to protect her.

We were both surprised to learn that he listened to the same radio shows we did. There were many nights he stayed with us sitting in the dark, eating colored popcorn and laughing at the comedians. He had a wonderful sense of humor and always had some kind of humorous anecdote about any situation.

I told you earlier about my ma's favorite joke... this one is Marvin's. It's about a guy and his neighbor who was helping him clean out his garage. The neighbor ran across an old beat-up boomerang and asked his friend if he wanted to keep it. "Hell no," he said, "It's been part of my junk for years." The neighbor asked him why he didn't throw it away like his other junk. He said, "Oh, I tried many times, but it keeps coming back."

Marvin's laid-back attitude brought a calmness that was having an effect on my ma. I could see, because of him, the weight of the world was slowly getting lighter. A thought kept entering my mind that he would be a wonderful person to take the place of Frank. I guess that my ma and Marvin thought the same thing, because she came to me one day and said, "Januscheck, he has asked me to marry him. He wants to be a husband to me and a father to you. What do you think about that?"

The words jumped out of my mouth. "MA! That would be great. Do it!"

Chapter 43

Marvin had never married and considered himself the typical bachelor. My ma learned that even if it was a long time since she heard from Frank, the law considered her a married woman. In order to remarry she would have to get a spousal abandonment document signed by a city judge. They called it an absentee divorce. It was too complicated for me to understand, so I left it up to them to work things out. It took a long time to find someone they could afford to handle the necessary legal steps. They finally ran across a young lawyer who was just starting in the judicial courts and needed not only money, but also experience. They worked out a deal to make monthly payments toward his fee.

As I recall it, she had to run a weekly notice in the local paper for six months. The wording in the ad asked if anyone knows or has any information as to the whereabouts of Frank Dramski, they should get in touch with a Detective Roth. The ad gave the telephone number of his office. The ads and the young lawyer's fee ran up to a sizable bill. My ma said the price to end her marriage to Frank would be well worth it... ten-fold.

It was great news to hear from the lawyer that after the six months, no one called or left any messages. He said a judge had just signed the papers and she could come and get them. The time it took to place the ads in the paper, get the release from Detective Roth and a judge to grant the divorce papers, took one full year.

Without wasting time, we went to the see the priest at St. Stanislaus, the Polish church that my ma and Frank were married in.

He had seen her many times, either in church or at one of their many socials. He assumed that Marvin was her husband, because Frank had never visited the church. When she told him they wanted to get married, the priest stood up and just stared at her with a puzzled look. He asked, "Why would you want to take your vows over again so soon?"

When she told him that Marvin wasn't Frank, he threw his hands up in the air and said, "Francis, start all over again, I'm thoroughly confused." She then explained that Marvin wasn't her husband and that her husband Frank had been missing for many years. She showed him the spousal document and the signed divorce papers by a judge. It was then that the priest laid the bomb on her. "Francis, I'm afraid the church cannot give its blessing. In the eyes of the church, you still have a husband and anything short of a death certificate would free you of that fact. Until you have that certificate, you cannot be married in this church." As the priest's words were sinking in, I could see the weight of the world climbing back up on my ma's shoulders. He also followed with the warning that if she were to wed outside the church, she would in fact be living in sin. It would be adultery in the eyes of the church. He also stated she would not be able to come for confession, nor would she be able to receive the Holy Eucharist.

I know this is hard to believe, but at the time, the Pastor of the church was a cruel tyrannical man of the cloth, who ran his church as he saw fit.

Knowing my ma, I could understand how demoralizing that information affected her. She and Marvin even went to see the Bishop, hoping he could do anything for them. He said the church tries not to interfere with a pastor's running of his parish and couldn't make any exceptions no matter what the circumstances. My ma said she wouldn't do anything that would keep her from receiving those Sacraments... so there will be no wedding.

At the supper table the next night, Marvin presented a plan. He asked her if it would be all right to get married by the Justice Of The Peace, then when the church was satisfied that Frank was deceased, they would immediately have a church wedding. I said, "Marvin, it's a great idea, but what if Frank would suddenly show up?" He was quick to state, "Your mother has legal divorce papers, so we'll cross that bridge if it ever comes to that." My ma agreed to give it some deep soul searching and pray for guidance. I never thought she would ever accept that idea, but after many telephone calls to Aunt Helen and weeks of praying to God to forgive her, she consented. The Lord is an understanding God and will forgive me when I can go for confession again. "Sometimes we have to do things to survive." I remember her saying those words so many times before.

Chapter 44

A month later in a ceremony at the courthouse performed by the Justice of the Peace, my ma and Marvin said, "I do." Aunt Helen, Uncle Steve and I witnessed the wedding. The celebration was a fabulous dinner held in the elegant Spaulding Hotel in downtown… oops, I almost said the name of the city again. The hotel was host to many famous people that visited the area. To name a few: President William McKinley, Woodrow Wilson, Steven Douglas and William Jennings Bryan also

made the Spaulding Hotel their place to stay. In the entertainment field Johnny Cash, while staying at the hotel, wrote a song about the town. The leading actress at that time was the famous Ann Baxter, who adopted the city as her home.

The wedding table in the dining room of the plush hotel was ready when we arrived. There were ice buckets of champagne, trays of appetizing hors d'œuvres, followed by a prime rib roast, which was carved and served by the chef himself. The way the waiters stood by our table with their towels draped over their arms, reminded me of the time when my pal Blub and I ate in the officer's quarters at the army base in Indianapolis.

The serving of a three-tiered wedding cake with the little bride and groom dolls, topped off the dinner. As we were enjoying the cake, a strolling violin player came over to our table and played request numbers. My ma and I tested his musical ability by requesting songs we had on the rolls of our player piano.

If you are wondering how the bride and groom could have afforded it, well, again, it was a present from Uncle Steve and Aunt Helen.

Chapter 45

The wedding changed our living conditions immediately. The things that needed replacing were now in an affordable range. With the pooling of their income and monthly payment plans, my parents could now upgrade household appliances. The first thing to go was the cast iron stove, Old Lucifer. In its place, on brand new linoleum, stood a modern oil-burning heater. The oil came in through a copper tube from a tank in the back of the house. This eliminated lugging heavy buckets of coal all the way from the alley. The oil company checked and filled the tank whenever needed. There were dials behind the stove that controlled the desired amount of heat and a flat plate for heating water. The temperature level was always constant, especially up in my bedroom. It kept me cozy warm, and I never had to use my featherbed again. The kitchen was up to date with the arrival of an electric refrigerator. The only thing I missed about the old icebox was the iceman. It was a great treat for us kids to jump up in the back of his truck and find chips of ice that flew off the block as he hacked away with his pick. With the new refrigerator, we made our own ice cubes and even Popsicles. We eliminated the problem of food spoiling in the antiquated icebox and saved on grocery bills. I was really looking forward to getting a hot water tank. Sponging the body with ice-cold water was shocking to the touch… especially my peepka!

There was a little ditty that went like this: "Once there was an iceman, who used to bring our ice. He was the nicest iceman whoever brought our ice. He came around so often, when my daddy wasn't there, that dad got rid of the icebox and bought a Frigidaire."

One of the biggest jobs for Marvin was sealing up the outside entrance to the cellar. Years of erosion made wide cracks around the steps leading down. It was through those cracks that rodents were coming in. In its place, he built a sunroom for my ma's ferns. It had windows on all three sides and her beautiful potted plants received the benefit of sunshine all day. Before closing that entrance, he built a controlled smudge-fire to drive out that rat, Diabel. Marvin was sure he had flushed out that ferocious beast and Diabel was now in some other cellar in the neighborhood. From all the stooping over he had to do, took a toll on his back. It was weeks before he could straighten up again and it even took longer for the lingering smell of the smudge-fire to fade away. He replaced the old island shelf with a new one and also the shelves that lined the outside walls. He believed it was behind the jars on those shelves, that Diabel would hide. When he finally sealed up the cellar, my ma started storing perishable items again. In spite of all the tedious work, it didn't take long before we were still finding gunnysacks ripped open. It was discouraging that there was still some animal in our cellar and we had no doubt who it was.

Marvin was proving to be the husband my ma so richly deserved. I could see how much she was learning to love him and I too had held great admiration for him. It was a wonderful tribute to her when he built colorful cement birdbaths for her flower garden. I was surprised when he asked me if I had some extra marbles he could have. I was the cities marble champion three years in a row and accumulated quite a large collection. There were times when a mother came to our front door with her son in tears, asking my ma to make me give her kid's marbles back. Usually their sad story was that the marbles were his birthday or Christmas present. My ma would say, "If your son would have won, would you have him give the marbles back? I think not." She would then follow with, "My son beat him fair and square… so he keeps the winnings."

"Yes, but your boy is the city champion," she would plead.

"Well then, your boy should not have challenged him. Good-day Mrs." My ma never let it go at that. She asked me to make a better judgment as to the ability of my opponent. "But ma, the marbles are already in the ring before we even start shooting, so if they are stupid enough to keep losing, I have to answer their challenge."

In my senior year, they named me captain of our varsity baseball and basketball teams and only needed one more sport to receive a special honor jacket given to senior athletes who earned a letter in three sports. I thought I could make the golf team, because I found an old rusty five iron, back then called, a Niblick. I had so many marbles; I practiced hitting them over the fence from our front yard, into an undeveloped section of the cemetery. Years later, I learned that there was a heck of a lot more to golf than hitting marbles off a sand tee. I also learned old Digit Dugan was completely baffled, trying to figure out how the dirt in the cemetery could be unearthing chipped pieces of colorful agates. When I tried out for golf, I learned the school didn't supply a set of golf clubs, so only the rich kids with parents belonging to the Potawatomi Country Club were the ones that made the team.

I was past the marble playing age anyway and I told Marvin he could have them all. I had no idea why he would want marbles, until I saw two elaborate birdbaths completely adorned with multi-colored marbles inserted in the cement. What a beautiful sight seeing them among the flowers, while varieties of feathered friends flittered and splashed in the water.

Each night before I went to sleep, I would thank the Lord for Marvin and always include... please God don't have Frank come back.

Chapter 46

With a war brewing in Europe and the need for more steel, the mills in Gary, Indiana were adding more workers. The influx of men from the southern states was bursting the town at its seams. The population was growing and living accommodations were becoming very scarce. This caused many to settle in nearby cities and commute to the mills. Our city, which is only a short drive to the mills in Gary, was one of the towns most chosen. The banks were now starting to ease the qualifications on home loans and they were building many new houses, increasing our city's population. Because of this growth, the city announced that they would soon be developing more areas for gravesites. One of those vacant areas was right across the street from our house. My ma was very upset about the news, because that would mean more cars parking at the gate and the possibility of flowers stolen from her garden. On the other hand, I too was concerned about the loss of my driving range.

The city was not only opening up new lots, but also replacing old equipment with up-to-date machinery. This meant they were going to retire the foreman old Dig-it Dugan and have his mare, the Bitch, sold to make gum or glue or whatever they did with old nags.

It was not surprising waking up one Monday morning and seeing surveyors laying out the lots and water lines. What it all meant to me, was for the rest of the summer, it would interrupt my theater of entertainment. With all the equipment lying out in the open, the police would be making their periodic runs inside the cemetery grounds. As a result, the lovers would not be putting on their orgies for me. They would have to find somewhere else to park.

As it turned out, I wouldn't have the use of the telescope anyway. One of the priests at the church had a mother dying back in Poland and the church was holding an auction to raise money for his trip. My ma, in spite of the way the church handled her request to be married, gave the helmet and telescope for the auction. Aunt Helen and Uncle Steve could not believe that she would donate such treasured memorabilia. When we asked her why, she proudly stated, "Maybe the death of some soldier long ago could now help in sending a son to the bedside of his dying mother." Somehow, I knew that would be her reasoning.

There was one item in my grandfather's collection she said she would never give away, the notched-knife that trapped the opponent's sword. She said they could end up in the wrong hands and kill someone. "I think it is better for me to keep it here in the kitchen with the rest of my knives." I wanted to say, ya ma, but I bet it would have gotten the highest bid... but I didn't.

Chapter 47

One of the many problems my parents had was when they surveyed the north side of my grandfather's property; the new owners discovered that the corner of his unfinished building stood six inches over on their lot. The official letter from their lawyer stated the city would have to have the infringement corrected. It also stated that if not done by a certain date, they would remove it for them and a lien put on the property for the cost. Marvin contacted a number of companies that did that sort of work, but before they would even start the job, they required a large down payment. In spite of the little equity they had in the house, my ma somehow talked the bank into giving her a loan.

It didn't take long for the crew to arrive with their trucks and cranes and start setting the building over the required inches. When they finished, they left it on temporary blocks and we had to set the structure on a permanent foundation. With all the money from the loan used up, it would stay that way for a very long time.

When I saw the open spaces along the foundation, it gave me a great idea. I planned to crawl under and hide there on the nights we played Ditch. I kept that to myself and the following summer when they paired me up with Mildred, I told her I knew another good place to hide. Mildred always trusted my cleverness and when I told her it wasn't the cemetery this time, she followed my lead without any hesitation.

Taking her by the hand and with our flashlights turned off, we headed around my house into the back yard. When we reached the unfinished building, I quickly dropped down on my belly and started crawling under the opening in the foundation. I planned to only go under just far enough so that our shoes wouldn't be seen sticking out. As I crawled forward into the pitch darkness, I kept my arms stretched out in front of me, making sure the path ahead was clear of any obstruction. I only had a few more inches to go when my fingers touched something. I whispered to Mildred to wait a minute while I turned on my flashlight to see what it was. When the light beam hit the object, I was so shocked I bumped my head trying to back out. With a lump in my throat I yelled, "Mildred back up."

In a whispering voice she questioned, "Why Michael what's wrong?" I didn't answer her but forced her backwards out in the open. While we knelt there brushing the sand off our clothing, two beams of light came shining down and I heard that dreadful word for the first time... "CAPTURED!"

I never confessed to Mildred what caused me to panic for fear I wouldn't be her brave hero anymore. I couldn't tell her that the dead carcass of some animal scared the living daylights out of me. I wasn't very proud of myself either, but the sudden sight of a skull with large fangs and dark hallowed out eyes, only inches from my face, would have even scared Frankenstein's monster. When I told my ma what was under the building, she immediately called the city animal control.

The man that came out, said it was the carcass of some feline animal, probably a tomcat that had crawled under there to die. He also said that he had never seen a cat's head quite that large before.

I don't know if my ma ever gave any more thought about it, but I kept reliving the sight of that awful skull in many nightmares. We often wondered why we hadn't seen Dupa around the house for weeks and now we knew why.

After Frank had abandoned him, the cat seemed to change dramatically. He spent most of his time in the cemetery and never ate the food we laid out for him. We never saw him bringing his catches back home anymore either. She said he must be eating his prey elsewhere and that's why he won't touch his dishes. Her statement sounded quite feasible, but if he was eating, why was he losing weight and getting so scrawny looking? He also used to run at high speed across Barker Avenue and with one giant leap, clear the fence into the cemetery. Lately however he was walking very slowly, oblivious to the traffic that veered to miss him. He would no longer leap, but would enter the cemetery through the gaps in the fence. My theory about the mysterious skull… was a pet with love and devotion that started as a little kitten was suddenly left forlorn. The mummified creature with the hallowed out eyes and the long sharp fangs, was that of a cat named Dupa, who abandoned by the master he adored, crawled under the structure and there all alone in the darkness, died of a broken heart. Although I hated my stepfather Frank, I felt sorry for the cat. I knew my ma did too.

Chapter 48

It was on a Monday afternoon when I returned home from school, that I saw a police and coroner's car parked in an area just inside the cemetery fence. They were directly across the street from my house and I was curious as to what was going on. I hurriedly parked my bike and ran over to the gate only to find it padlocked. I walked around to where the men were gathered and climbed up on the fence. I wasn't the only one that was curious, because the whole neighborhood was on their way over.

When the police saw a crowd beginning to block traffic, they told us to go home and to read the report in the newspaper. I immediately ran across the street and up the stairs to my bedroom. I knew with the telescope, I would at least be able to see what they were doing. It never dawned on me until I got upstairs, that I did not have the telescope anymore. My ma had auctioned it off at the church. What I did notice though, was they were sifting sand around the area of the hole Mildred and I stumbled into playing Ditch. If someone else had fallen into it, why was the Coroner there?

I also remembered Dig-it had the sand replaced, because I made a special check to be sure. I didn't want to fall into it the next time we played Ditch. I was relieved to see the hole refilled.

The front-page headline read in bold letters, A SKELTON IS FOUND IN AN UNMARKED GRAVE. The paper reported that while digging the ditches for the water pipes, workers unearthed some bones, and immediately informed the cemetery officials. There was a possibility that they may have disturbed a hallowed grave. They told the crews to hold off until they analyzed the bones. It would not have been a surprise to me; that they could be the bones of someone's pet. There was evidence that people in the dark of night, were sneaking into the cemetery and burying their beloved animals.

When the coroner's office had finished examining the bones, they reported it was a human male. It was unfortunate that while digging with the heavy machinery, the brittle skull and extremities were crushed beyond any reconstruction. What was in perfect condition though, was the rib cage. This puzzled the police, because the tractor shovel never struck the torso, yet one rib was broken off and laid inside the ribcage. They described it as the fifth rib on the left side. They estimated the body to have been in that shallow grave for many years. The only clothing was summer underwear that had rotted so badly the company's label was unreadable. What the underwear indicated was someone buried it during the summer months. If it were in the colder months of the year, the man would have been wearing long johns.

I don't know if you ever heard of them. They had a convenient feature… a trap door in the back.

It didn't take long after the article hit the paper that Barker Avenue became a parade route. People were driving by to get a look at the site where they found the skeleton with the broken rib.

Chapter 49

With nothing to go on other than some crushed bones, left the police facing quite a problem. Who is he and was it a homicide? Could he have been killed somewhere else, then brought to the cemetery or did the murder take place right at that spot? The ribcage was another puzzle. If the tractor blade never touched it, then how did that one rib get broken? It was determined that it must have happened at the time of the killing. They reported the story in hundreds of newspapers throughout the state. A Chicago paper titled it "THE SKELETON WITH THE BROKEN RIB."

My Aunt Helen upon reading it immediately called my ma warning her that the police would soon be canvassing the neighborhood, asking questions about missing people. It is inevitable that they will want to question you about Frank. She and Uncle Steve were on their way to help corroborate any of her statements. They arrived the next morning just minutes ahead of the police.

The detective assigned to the case was, Herr Rudolph Von Krueger, also called, the 'Bulldog.' They called him that because of his reputation that once he got his teeth into a case, he would not let go until he solved it. He was a burley looking character that always wore a black pinstriped suit, white shirt and black tie. Everything he wore should have been a size larger; consequently, he never buttoned any of the uncomfortable areas; the suit coat around the waist, the last three buttons of his vest or his shirt at the collar. His black tie hung an inch or two from his neck and had the telltale signs of never protecting it whenever he stopped for a bowl of soup. From the way his belly hung over his belt, it looked like there were a lot of mashed potatoes, gravy, ice cream and cake devoured along with that bowl of soup. His features also had the resemblance of a bulldog. His back and shoulders went right up to his head. It didn't look like he had any neck at all. Even his face had the small snub-nose, situated between beady eyes that were always tearing. The most outstanding likeness to a bulldog was the jutting out of his lower jaw, where he chewed a juicy cigar butt constantly. I was amazed at the way he was able to shift that stub from one corner of his mouth to the other and all the while the maneuver was in progress, kept right on talking without interrupting his speech. If you can picture a black derby precariously perched on his head, you have Herr Rudolph Von Krueger... the 'Bulldog.'

His sloppy appearance in no way belied the sharp intelligence of his German heritage. He spent most of his life doing police work and was much respected in his field. His career started in the Chicago area where he climbed up the ladder from patrol officer to finally making Detective First Class. Krueger became a thorn in the side of many bad apples, one of which was the notorious Al Capone. He had the bulldogged determination to get those, as he called them, rats off the streets. He was constantly receiving threatening phone calls on his life. After living through several attempts at his assassination, his wife begged him to leave Illinois and find employment in a less volatile city.

At this time, our city was searching for someone to head a newly enlarged police department. Krueger spent many vacations with his family in our area and fell in love with the beautiful recreational facilities and the friendliness of its thirty-some thousand citizens. When he was approached by our city council, he took the offer. Krueger's assistant looked very young to have already earned the title of detective. He introduced him as Ellery. I never heard Krueger refer to him in any other way, but "my assistant, Ellery." I wondered what the odds would be that someday I'd find out his last name was... Queen. It later became public knowledge that Krueger did not want it known that Ellery was the son of his wife's sister. I thought about all the amount of nagging that must have taken place, getting Krueger to give his tall, thin-as-a-rail nephew, a position on the force.

They were in complete contrast to each other. Krueger was so overweight his clothing stretched to the very limits, while Ellery on the other hand, looked like his clothes had room enough for another him. By the way, he quickly agreed to every statement Krueger made, you could see that Ellery was in complete awe of his famous boss. Talk about a 'yes man,' Ellery's head was bobbing up and down so much it looked like one of those Bobble-Head dolls in the back window of many cars today.

I felt sorry for Ellery though. He was a good-looking kid that failed his first year in college and pressured into taking a job dealing with criminal apprehension. I don't think Ellery ever wanted to be in the field of criminology. You could tell the young detective was trying very hard to emulate his boss. Krueger demanded one restriction. It was that Ellery could not wear a black suit with pin stripes. That's where the Bulldog drew the line. To him pinstripes indicated rank. If you saw them together, you would swear some Hollywood-casting director dreamed up another Laurel and Hardy.

It didn't take long to see how the Bulldog got his reputation. The way he hurriedly jumped out of the car and rushed up to our front door was an indication he couldn't wait to get started. I didn't see him flash any search warrant, but marched right in asking questions. At this time, other police cars were arriving with cases of instruments. They started spreading out to all parts of our property. Krueger did the questioning and the bobble-head Ellery, with pad in hand, was poised to take down our statements. I don't think the Bulldog trusted Ellery too much, because he was always turning to ask, "Did you write that down, boy?"

Krueger asked for Marvin, but I told him, he was working over at the prison. He said, "Tell him to come down to the station so I can question him alone." It was quite evident that Krueger was already coming up with the idea that Frank was the skeleton and Marvin had something to do with his demise. Aunt Helen and Uncle Steve both agreed that Krueger's line of thinking was that Frank came back still claiming to be the lawful husband and my parents had decided to get rid of him. I said, "If the Bulldog thought my ma would take part in anything like that... he's barking up the wrong tree." (I'm sorry... no pun intended.)

All the while, the interrogation was taking place; Krueger's men were going over the property inside and out, searching for evidence. They got all excited when they discovered the chopping block with the dark brown stains. They immediately rushed it to the lab downtown in hopes of finding traces of human blood. I could have assured them that the only blood they were going to find came from hundreds of unfortunate non-egg laying hens. They must have thoroughly examined the block because you could see they cut three inches of the top portion away, which I am sure disappointed thousands of flies impatiently waiting for its return.

When Marvin went to the station for questioning, they held him for half a day. On returning home he summed up the whole inquest with, as he put it, "They think there is a possibility I had eliminated Frank so I could marry your mother." That idea was so preposterous to me, I could not stop laughing. My ma's response was that Krueger is just doing his job and they had to consider all possibilities. I couldn't see how she could be so understanding, under these trying circumstances.

Krueger's pursuit was relentless. He and his men were at our house for days on end. They searched from early morning to late in the afternoon. The only time they took a break was when Krueger had to stop for his bowl of soup. You could see Krueger was getting very frustrated with the lack of progress toward solving the mystery. The disappearance of Frank and a skeleton found in the cemetery right across from our house, kept the Bulldog pursuing his theory that the answer is at our house. He had his teeth locked in on that idea and as he was noted for, wasn't going to let go. The thought that my ma would ever have anything to do with breaking God's commandment, Thou Shalt Not Kill, was causing me to dislike him very much.

We informed Ellery that Frank wasn't the only person who vanished. There was also a Mr. Melon and Mr. Balan. Their departure was in such a hurry, they left personal possessions behind including what was left of the month's pro-rated rent. We told him about all the fighting they did and both of them worked for Dig-it in the cemetery. There was also Mr. Washington; a Black man who worked with them, that also vanished. Whatever became of him? We never saw him after we came back from visiting the Chicago World's Fair. My ma had gathered clothing left behind from Uncle Steve and was waiting to get Mr. Washington's measurements. No one knew the tremendous frustration I was going through. I had a good idea what happened to Frank, because I witnessed his audition with Hilda that night in the cemetery. If I did tell what I saw, who would ever believe it; especially coming from a boy whose mother was a prime suspect.

Chapter 50

The surprising discovery of a skeleton across the street and Detective Krueger's intense suspicion that my ma and Marvin had something to do with it, was affecting her health. She started getting painful headaches that would often occur late at night, long after I had gone to bed. I awoke one time with the sounds of her moaning and groaning and went down the stairs to see if I could comfort her. Marvin had been working the night shift, so it was up to me to see what I could do. What I saw almost tore my heart out. She was pacing from one room to the other, holding her hands to her temples, praying in Polish to God, asking for some relief. I knew it was God she was talking to, because I understood the Polish word Bog means God. I said, "Ma, let me get you an aspirin or some Alka Seltzer."

"Oh I've tried all those things, Januscheck, but nothing helps. The only thing that seems to ease the pain is when I put pressure on my temples. God must have answered her prayers through me, because I got the idea of tying something around her head to take the place of her hands. I soaked the red bandana I used for Huckleberry Finn in cold water and tied it very tightly around her forehead. I then stuck two ice cubes under the bandana, one at each temple. We sat on the edge of her bed and as the ice cubes were melting, I kept twisting the knot to keep the pressure constant. Before the ice cubes melted, I could see that her pain had subsided. She laid back on her pillow in complete exhaustion and fell into a sound peaceful sleep. I was proud I could bring her some comfort in return for all the times she eased my suffering. The touch of her hand always gave me comfort and I still believe to this day, her touch was that of an angel.

I informed Aunt Helen that I thought the investigation was affecting my ma's health; causing her terrible headaches to return. She said, "Maybe so, Michael, but there could be another reason for them. You see your mother hasn't been able to go to confession because of her marriage to Marvin and believes each day she is committing adultery. Knowing Francis, the extreme torment she's going through is affecting her mental health. I'm sure if she had known the church would take so long to end its restriction, she would never have gone along with the wedding. Your mother wants to go to confession, receive her penitence and ask God to forgive her. Something concerns me much more than that, Michael, it's the frightening thought your Grandma Sophie also suffered with severe headaches."

It seemed strange, but like my ma, I too was suddenly having physical problems. It was a series of painful stomach cramps. My abs would tighten up just like the cramps people get in their thighs or hamstring muscles. The pain was so great; at times, it would render me immobilized. The only way I got some relief was to lie on my back, pull my knees up to my chest, put my arms around my legs and squeeze with all my might. This method didn't stop the cramping, but helped me stand the pain until the cramps finally subsided.

I never told my ma about the cramps, because I didn't want to give her another reason to bring on a migraine. I could always tell when those cramps were coming on. They would start out very lightly at first, and then kept getting stronger until I felt like my stomach muscles were in a vise. I discovered that I could ease the pain somewhat by softly tickling around my stomach area. This action worked for a while, but soon lost its soothing effect. With a little more experimenting I started tickling myself lower and lower on my body, until I discovered the part that tickled the most and helped in stemming the pain… my peepka.

My ma told me never to play with it, but maybe if she knew it was making me feel better, she would have another use for it. I also figured that if I wasn't thinking anything dirty while I was massaging it, then it wouldn't be self-gratification, thus not a sin. I guess the inevitable had to happen.

It was on a Saturday night after taking my bath and lying on the bed, that I felt the cramps coming on. They seemed to be coming on stronger and faster than ever before. The harder the cramping, the faster I tickled. For a time I thought I would have to go back to bringing my knees up to my chest, but suddenly I felt a surge of pumping contractions in my groin area. The cramping subsided and relief calmed my body. As I lay there sweating and breathing heavily, I discovered that my fingers were wet and very sticky. I immediately sat on the edge of the bed and looked down at my peepka. I had mixed emotions for what I had just done. Was it for medical reasons or did I do something to make my ma ashamed of me? With tears in my eyes, I decided to deal with it later. I knew from hearing the 'older guys' talking about sex, that I must have had my first real orgasm. My problem now was that I had to go downstairs to wash off the mess it made. The next problem was walking past my ma who was sitting at the dining room table playing solitaire. I felt sure she would have that mother instinct that her boy needed help and would stop me, to ask if I was all right. I dreaded the thought of standing in front of her with my peepka pushing out the material of the bathrobe. It was a stroke of luck she was so engrossed in her card game, she never even looked up. Then there was also the problem of secretively sneaking the hot water kettle off the stove into the bathroom. If my ma saw me, she would certainly ask why, after just taking a bath, I would need more hot water.

To play it safe I didn't get the kettle, but used the water from the bathroom faucet. The shock of washing my tender peepka with ice-cold water was an experience I will never forget. It was then I learned if you wanted to get the stiffness out, just throw cold water on it. From that time on whenever I felt the cramps were starting, I tickled my peepka believing I was doing it for medicinal reasons. I didn't think it was a sin and never told anyone about it; not even the Priest at confession. I couldn't admit to myself that I was finally taking Snort's advice and whacking it.

My rationalizing that tickling my peepka was for medicinal purposes soon wore off. I had to stop touching it with my bare hands, so I used my ingenuity and devised another way to answer my problem. I thought of wearing a condom or rubber, but how was I going to buy them. I didn't think a druggist sold condoms to kids my age and where was I going to hide them if he did. Another great concern was how and where I could dispose of the used ones. I had the idea of flushing them down the toilet, but the thought of my ma catching me in the act would be, to say the least, a frightening experience. I even had a terrible nightmare about it. I dreamt that our toilet plugged up and my ma used the old plunger to free the water. While in the process of dislodging the problem, a bunch of used Trojans came floating to the top. I dropped that thought, 'pronto'. I did come up with a plan however, that I used for quite some time. Whenever I massaged my peepka, I draped it with one of my sweat socks that was destined for the washing machine and in that way I wouldn't be touching it with my hand. I don't think my ma ever wondered why some of the tips of my socks were stuck together. My idea of using sweat socks to whack in seemed to do the trick. It may have been just a coincidence, but I never had another attack of cramps after that. It was fortunate for me, because I was developing into quite an athlete.

Chapter 51

Aunt Helen's concern for my ma's migraines made a lot of sense, but I felt there was another reason. I was sure that Bulldog Krueger's persistence and constant hounding was stretching her patience to the brink of a nervous breakdown. I wondered if he just couldn't admit to himself that he was headed down the wrong road and his suspicions weren't getting him anywhere. I'm sure he feared his reputation was being tarnished. This was the first real big case since coming to our city and every newspaper in Chicago was carrying the story. I'm sure he was well aware of his cronies following the case. If Krueger had some new facts, I wondered if he would leave my ma alone.

With that thought in mind, I started racking my brain for something we hadn't told him in our interrogations. I couldn't understand why he wasn't following up on the information we gave Ellery about the three men who also vanished suddenly and why could it only be Frank's skeleton.

There was one important thing that Krueger never heard. It was about seeing Frank and Hilda in the cemetery that night and I believed they were planning to steal the Wolinski fortune. It was my secret, but maybe if I confided in him to keep it between us, he would agree. Thinking it would be better to talk to him alone; I called and asked to see him, because I had new information. The next day I biked downtown to the courthouse.

There are no words in my vocabulary that could accurately relate the experience of walking into the Bulldog's office. The stench from stale cigars was so strong; I got a whiff of it ten feet before I reached the door. It was permeating the whole area. I didn't know how long I'd be able to stay in that environment without getting sick to my stomach. It must have been his lunch hour, because there was still some soup left in the bowl on his desk. He asked if I could make my visit as short as possible, which I was already contemplating.

He was first to speak. "Come in, son, and tell me what you have on your mind." His statement didn't have that sternness that it did at our house. I thought that maybe the soup made him a little more humane. I was glad of that, because I always felt uneasy in his presence. In fact, I was so nervous my knees wouldn't stop shaking. He said, "If you don't mind, I'll keep eating while you talk. My lunch hour seems to go by so fast." I wished he hadn't gone on eating, because along with the smell that was gagging me, I noticed cigar juice in the corners of his mouth as he slurped his soup. I'm sure by this time my complexion was turning a pea green.

"Mr. Krueger, if I told you a secret that I never divulged at the inquest and it helped you in solving the mystery, would you help me keep it?"

"Well son, before I can promise you anything, I'll have to hear what it is. I don't think there is any doubt in anyone's mind, that the case has stalled and I need more information to continue. If you're secret sheds new light, you can have my word on it." I had a feeling I could trust him, because I once heard at a pow-wow, if a guy has tobacco juice running down both corners of his mouth, it means he's on the level.

I proceeded to tell him about the telescope I used to scan the cemetery. I also told him about seeing my stepfather Frank and Mrs.

Wolinski making love. I informed him that it was shortly after that the robbery at Stash's Tavern took place.

"Mr. Krueger, Frank hasn't been home since."

"Well son, that wasn't exactly what I was hoping to hear from you; now I don't have any idea who the skeleton could be."

"Yes you do Mr. Krueger. It could be one of the other three men that vanished."

"Three men vanished… what other three, son?"

"The men we told your assistant about." Krueger immediately pulled back the drawer in his desk and took out what looked like the pad Ellery was using the day we gave him all the information. I could see the Bulldog was all excited, because the cigar stub was on its journey moving rapidly from side to side.

"DAMN THAT ELLERY," he shouted as he slammed the book down on his desk. "If I don't stay on him every second, that kid would never write anything down at his interviews." I'll tell you what son, if you give me the names and information on the men, I'll get right on it today."

I figured by the time I gave all that information, it would take at least another twenty minutes before I could get back to taking a full breath of fresh air again. His promise to follow up on my information, helped me endure the smoke that was burning my youthful lungs and hurriedly said, "Mr. Krueger, all three men worked at the cemetery under a foreman named Dugan. You can get all the information on them at the cemetery pump-house.

I was proud as a peacock when he patted me on the back and thanked me for the new leads. As I was leaving the office, he shook my hand and said, "You love your mother very much, don't you lad?"

I said, "Yes sir, Mr. Krueger, and some day I would like to tell the whole world just how much."

Maybe I already have started with you, my passenger.

In all my excitement on the way home, a sudden thought interrupted my exalted feelings. If the area was once a farm, why couldn't the bones be that of the farmer's family, or for that matter, a farm hand or an Indian worker? It couldn't be an Indian, because they didn't wear clothing that featured a convenient trap door. I hated myself for not coming up with that scenario back at the police station. I finally decided to let the Bulldog work on what I did give him and save the other possibilities for later.

Chapter 52

T he new leads I gave to Krueger did the trick. A whole week had gone by without a trip to our house by the detective or his men. The fact that we didn't hear from him, led me to believe he was currently on a new theory as to who the skeleton might be. I was relieved to see a headline in the local newspaper that stated... *NEW LEADS IN SKELETON MYSTERY*. It reported there were three missing men that had worked at the cemetery. All three had suddenly vanished at the same time. Krueger

went on to say he believed one of them was murdered and the crime was committed right on that spot they found the skeleton. From what he learned, one of the three men or even two could be the killer or killers. I felt elated to see that the Bulldog was really on a roll, so to speak. He even offered a theory as to what may have happened. He believed that the victim was probably struck by a pickaxe with such force that on its way to piercing the heart, the pointed end also broke off a rib.

Now that Krueger was pursuing the case in a different direction relieved us, especially my ma. I don't remember her suffering any migraines after that. I knew Krueger's job was going to be very complicated. Do the bones belong to Mr. Washington, murdered by Mr. Melon, or did Mr. Balan and Mr. Melon together kill Mr. Washington? Then again, is the skeleton that of Mr. Melon, killed by Mr. Balan or is it Mr. Balan's skeleton, murdered by Mr. Melon. Then there is a possibility that Mr. Washington killed Mr. Melon or Mr. Balan, if so, where is the surviving Mr. Melon, Mr. Balan or Mr. Washington? The many possibilities were certainly going to give the Bulldog the fits. I pitied the boxes of cigars he would chew to hell in the process.

Chapter 53

I t was quite a relief to know that all the police work was now taking place on the other side of the cemetery fence and not at our residence. Aunt Helen returned to Chicago and the three of us went back to our normal lives again. For many days on end, my ma and I sat on the porch watching the men in the cemetery sifting through the sand in search of more evidence. It was reported that in order for the searching to continue, they were going to develop the new gravesites in some other area of the cemetery.

The searching went on for many weeks, but little by little, the action dwindled down until there was none at all. For many months, there wasn't anything new about the case. The last article printed, stated that Detective Krueger was filing it away as, UNSOLVED. He said it didn't qualify for an FBI involvement and with a limited staff; he didn't have manpower or capital to trace the leads. He said the only thing he learned about the three suspects, was that they came from Mississippi and that two of them at one time had connections with the KKK. It was easy for me to figure out which two they were. I was quite sure Mr. Washington would never have been welcomed into the Klu Klux Klan. I remember how relieved we were, when they filed the mystery of THE SKELETON WITH THE BROKEN RIB away as the city's own 'Cold Case.' In fact, Marvin, while sitting at the supper table, said he considers Frank dead, and never to return. I wasn't quite convinced of that, because only I knew he could be squandering the Wolinski fortune. I reminded them, I was nearing my high school graduation and if they were going to decide on a college, they would have to start now.

They agreed and from then on, my ma covered the dining room table with college pamphlets, most of which were about Notre Dame. When I was very young she took me to visit the town of South Bend Indiana, where the famous college is located. Notre Dame wasn't noted only for great football teams, but the success of its graduates entering the business world. I wanted to please her, but my future plan was to study plant life. I knew she would help me with my studies. She had already taught me a lot about the wonders of nature and was pleased at my choice. I decided I would rather work with Mother Nature, giving life to things, than be a career soldier that may have to end one. I searched for colleges offering classes in biology. We tried to find one in our state, so I could be nearer to home.

I couldn't get the thought out of my mind, that here we were making plans for the future, but what would the Gypsy fortuneteller's reaction be? Well, as it turned out, she would have roared with laughter again.

Chapter 54

I made the varsity team in basketball and baseball three years in a row and they voted me captain of both teams in my senior year. Our basketball team was popular throughout the state for its 'toy guards,' Jimmy Dry and me. Although we were both only five-foot-seven, we were deadly from way out beyond the thirty-foot circle. If they had the three-point system back then, no one would have beaten us. Our team was one of five favored to win the Indiana state championship. Although we defeated some of the best teams and tied for the conference championship, we never made it past the sectionals. Our team had a devastating upset loss by a little farm school called Rolling Prairie. There was a statement made by a devoted fan, which predicted our high school team would never win the state championship until there were some black players. I don't remember who he was, but he must have used the Gypsy woman's crystal ball. In 1966, our school, with the help of black players brought the coveted trophy back from the state capital. They defeated Indianapolis Tech, 63-52.

Our baseball team fared a lot better, however. We won the state championship with relative ease. I wasn't only the captain, but also the star pitcher. I was lucky to have a great arm. My fastball had an upward movement as it reached the hitting area and my curve or slider as they call it now, had the potential for a big league future. My ma never missed any of the home games, all three years. She was a great fan and I could hear her penetrating shouts of encouragement above the roar of the crowd. I remember one basketball game that went into three overtimes. It finally ended in a sudden death playoff, when I scored the winning basket from the middle of the court. Our neighbors sitting alongside my ma said when she got up to leave; they noticed the bench was wet. I wondered if she did that at every game. I was proud to be her hero. As I look back on it, those were the happiest years of my youth and went by the fastest too.

I never dated in all my years in school, even prom night. It wasn't that I didn't have a lot of opportunities. Girls were always handing me notes or telephoning with invitations to a party or dance. In return, I would either give them some excuse or just ignore the notes. Why I stayed away from girls, I will never know. Maybe it was because I was afraid of succumbing to sexual temptations by 'shoestrings.' I had always planned on waiting until I was married. There were rumors among the girls that maybe I was queer. How could they believe someone like me, a star athlete, was a sissy? That was one of the names they gave those who are sexually different. Men were queers or sissies. Women were tomboys, dykes, or bitches. Today the world is more understanding. I think I was the only male senior in school that was still a virgin. That is, if the sweat socks don't count!

One time at a pow-wow, an older guy started boasting about having sex since he was a senior in high school. He said it was with a teacher at our high school. He said, "Whenever she had designs on a certain student, she would make sure he got the front desk on the side of the room along the windows. Then at an opportune time, she would pull out the lower drawer of her desk, place her foot up on it and lean back pretending to be reading. With her leg up like that, I could see she wasn't wearing anything underneath. There were times I caught her peeking over her book, making sure I was taking in all the sights.

She asked me if I would like to stay after school one Friday to help her clean the blackboards. It didn't take too many Fridays till she was locking the door and taking me to the back of the room for sex. I tried to call her many times after I graduated, but she keeps hanging up. I guess she only dug high school seniors." He told us her name, which I won't divulge for obvious reasons. He said if we ever have her for a teacher, watch what desk she gives you. I can see by the look on your face, you know what is coming... well you're right!

When I finally reached my senior year, I was surprised she was still teaching. They assigned me to her room and was completely stunned by her youthful features. Evidently, sex with a teen-ager was her 'fountain of youth.' The first day was 'getting acquainted' day and we sat wherever we wanted to. The next day everyone had a desk assigned. I was shocked to find that my desk was the very same one that the older guy was talking about, the front desk by the windows. After a week had gone by and nothing out of the ordinary happened, I had the feeling that the story he told was just another older guy trying to inflate his ego. It wasn't until the third week of school that I finally got the view displayed for me. Although the light from the large windows was sufficient, all I could see was she wasn't wearing any lace panties.

She began asking me if I would like to stay and clean the blackboards on Fridays. I kept making excuses that I had to go to the gym for practice. I thought if I kept turning her down, she would stop asking. I soon found she had other ways of getting what she wanted. She informed me one Friday, that I had to stay after school. She said that it was a detention for chewing gum in class. I could tell by her false accusation, she had a plan. What puzzled me was another student got the same order to stay. How could any illicit sex happen, when there were two classmates and the other one a girl? That situation cleared, when the teacher told Betty to go home. I knew then, she had me alone and trapped. Not knowing what else to do, I raised my hand. "What is it, Michael?"

"Can I go home too," I asked?

She answered with a soft pleasing voice, "Would you clean the blackboards for me first?"

I hadn't the slightest idea how her ploy included cleaning the blackboards, but boy, did I find out. Without hesitating, I dashed up, grabbed the eraser and frantically started wiping the chalked figures. My action was with the job at hand, but my mind was on what the teacher was doing behind me. I heard the words "don't move, Michael," as she pushed me roughly against the blackboard. With my arms extended above my head, I felt like a captive. I had the strength to break away anytime I wanted to. What surprised me is that I didn't make an effort to do so. I just stood there and waited to see what she would do next. It didn't take long to find out. It started with her question, "Have you ever had sex with a woman, Michael, honey"? I tried to speak, but was still stunned by her actions. She went on to add; "Well, you are going to now, dear." With those words, I felt her hand come searching around my legs, groping for the buttons on my fly. "Let me see how big our Michael is getting to be," she giggled. With that statement, I felt one button pop loose.

For the life of me, I couldn't believe I was allowing this rape to happen, but was more concerned she got a single. It was after her double and triple, I felt her entire hand enter my pants. "You'll love what I'm going to do to you next, Michael, sweetheart." It was the word, sweetheart, that brought me back to reality. There was only one person I could ever be a sweetheart to, and that one, I'm sure you know by now... my ma. By the time I returned to reality, my teacher was down on her knees in front of me. My pants were completely open, exposing everything. Pushing her head back, I grabbed my pants, pulled them up and headed for the door. "Wait awhile Michael, where are you going'? "To the toilet to pee," I informed her. "But we are just getting started, sweetheart." With the word, sweetheart ringing in my ears, I dashed for the door, unlocked it and ran to my bike my mother bought me for my first communion. While I was on my bike, I felt air entering my groin area. Looking down, I saw that my fly was completely open. When I stopped to button up, I noticed all four buttons were loose. How would I be able to face the 'older guys'? No one was ever able to score a home run on me and now of all people, a woman did it. What is even worse, a 'shoe-string.' I never told anyone what the teacher did. That would be squealing and back then, no kid wanted anyone to call him or her a squealer, because in the movies, James Cagney called them dirty rats and shot them.

It was no surprise to me that when I came to class on Monday, she had moved my desk to the back of the room. I had to admit it left me with mixed emotions. Did I miss a chance to learn about sex from an expert, or be glad I hadn't sinned with a woman fifteen years my elder and of all people, a respected schoolteacher.

I thought you would be surprised to hear that teacher and student sex was even happening as far back as the thirties.

Chapter 55

I couldn't get over how great life had become. Here I was celebrating a time in my life with a stepfather I have grown to admire and respect. I had no fear that after all these years Frank would ever show up and cause trouble.

The next visit from my Aunt Helen and Uncle Steve was for my graduation. After the ceremonies, they treated my ma, Marvin and me to another one of those fabulous dinners at the Spaulding Hotel. This time however, I could have one glass of champagne and raised it on high when Uncle Steve gave a toast to all my accomplishments. They presented me with my first wristwatch, a beautiful Gruen model with an expandable band. It also had an inscription engraved on the back… TO OUR MICHAEL. My ma wanted my aunt and uncle to stay longer, but Steve had to get right back to his office and they left the next day. My ma was quite disappointed, because she was planning one of her own extravagant meals at home.

"Gee ma; hasn't there been enough celebrating because of my diploma?"

"No Michael, I want to show my appreciation for your good work at school. It was the first time she ever called me Michael and I was a little surprised when I heard her say it. I knew then she was starting to see me as a young man and Januscheck was no longer appropriate. I wanted to tell her that no matter how old I get, in my heart I will always be her little Januscheck.

Whenever she cooked one of her elaborate meals, it took three days of preparation. I helped her as much as I could, which meant trips down in the cellar for jars of pickles, mushrooms, peaches and any other things she needed. She had planned to have the meal on Sunday, which meant she would be starting the preparations in the middle of the week. It was on Friday that she asked me to go down to the cellar to bring up the preserves. She told me what jars she wanted and on what shelf I would find them. All I could think of at the time was, here I go again, down in the dungeon where that damn rat Diabel made his kingdom.

With my heart racing and beads of sweat forming on my forehead, I approached the cellar door. I paused for a second to build up enough courage to start down those squeaky stairs. She said when I reached the cellar floor; I should turn right and go to the east wall to find the jars. I was hoping that Marvin had smoked Diabel out and he was now in some neighbor's cellar, giving them fits. A frightful thought crossed my mind, if he drove him away, what was tearing the holes in our gunnysacks? I tried to convince myself that being a great athlete, I ought to be able to face any rodents no matter how large and fierce they may be. I knew Diabel wouldn't attack as long as he felt safe and didn't feel threatened. It was only when he was cornered that he attacked. As I reluctantly sneaked down the steps, I wondered if I would ever have made a brave soldier.

To warn Diabel someone was coming, I flipped on the light down below. I paused at each step, straining my ears for any sound from the beast. Once I reached the floor of the dimly lit, musty smelling dungeon, I raced as fast as I could to get my errand done. I didn't want to spend any more time down there than I had to. I saw the jars my ma wanted, but had to remove a few to get at them.

What happened next was so sudden; I didn't have time to duck. A creature with two fiery red eyes darted out at me, screeching and hissing as it attached itself to my face. I felt the vicious claws digging into my flesh as it drove me back into the island shelf. I tore the animal away and flung it as hard as I could against the cement wall; so hard, I heard a popping sound as the last breath came out of Diabel's body. The sudden attack and struggle with the vicious rat left me weak and with a shoulder throbbing painfully from hurling Diabel against the wall. I stayed there on my knees waiting to regain my composure.

When I started to get up, I discovered during the attack, I had staggered backwards into the island shelves, causing one of the special pickle jars to come crashing down. I knew how important the pickles were to my ma, so I started to gather them up to see if she could still use them. I had to hurry, because the scratches were burning like hell and I had to get upstairs so my ma could doctor them. I had just about gathered up all the pickles, when I noticed something that didn't look like a pickle at all, but rather like a Bratwurst. Oh Ho, did I discover my ma's secret for giving her dill pickles that unique flavor and won all those blue ribbons. I wanted to pick it up and examine it, but it looked so weird I didn't want to touch it. With the use of another pickle, I rolled the grayish looking thing repeatedly, which was difficult to do, because it was limp and mushy. I couldn't determine exactly what it was just by rolling it, so I picked it up for a closer examination. I discovered that each end of the strange thing was tied with catgut. When the jar crashed on the floor, one end broke open. By now, my curiosity had piqued to the point where I just had to examine it even further. I rolled back the outer casing on the open end and what I saw made me quickly fling it back to the floor. I knelt there for a second looking at it in disbelief. Did I really see what I thought I saw? After all, my eyes were blurry from the sweat and blood running down my forehead. I wiped across my eyes with the sleeve of my shirt and picked it up for a more thorough look. This time however, I pulled the casing back even further and exposed of all things, the head of a penis! What in the name of heaven was it doing in my ma's pickle jar and whom did it belong to? The more I handled it, the more repulsive it became. I was about to take it upstairs when to my horror I noticed that a small tip of the penis was missing. Suddenly like a bolt of lightning, it hit me and the name spurted from my mouth, FRANK! Oh my God, was this Frank's penis? If so, how in the world did Frank's penis become one of my ma's pickles?

Chapter 56

I've had nightmares before, but nothing like the one I was having in that cellar. I was hoping to awake and realize it was only a dream. That chance was shattered by the sound of my Ma's voice coming from the top of the stairs.

"Michael, are you all right?" I knew then, all this was for real and I would have to go up and confront her about my discovery.

"I'm okay ma, stay there, I'll be right up." I wanted to wait until my head cleared, so I could figure out how I was going to start. I had to hurry, because the sweat was running into the scratches, making the pinching become more unbearable. I knew I had to think fast. It was evident that she knew something about Frank's disappearance. My ma was the person that canned the pickles and stuffed the jars. I decided there was only one way to handle it and that was to come right out and ask her, 'point blank.' I left the penis on the cellar floor along with Diabel's carcass and made my way back up the stairs. I still couldn't believe what had taken place. Did she cut it off in punishment for all the chasing around he did with other women? She would never be that cruel to perform such a gruesome act. I couldn't erase the picture however, of seeing her chopping off the head of the chicken or slicing across the head of that pretty white duck. Then there was that quotation she lived by... "Sometimes we have to do things to survive." I couldn't wait to hear how that statement would be appropriate to lopping off someone's peepka. I had to question her now, while we were alone.

When she saw the scratches on my forehead and the blood

running down into my eyes, she ran to the bathroom for the iodine. That was the favorite antibiotic medicine used in those days. It always did the job, but the application usually stung more than the wound. I sat on the kitchen chair while she doctored the deep gouges caused by Diabel's sharp claws. For the first time, I found myself looking up at my ma's face and not seeing her as a kind gentle person, but maybe the face of a killer…

It took all the courage I could muster-up to do what I had to. I reached up, grabbed her hand, and said, "Just a minute ma, I have to ask you something." With her free hand, she cupped my chin, lifted my face so she could look directly into my eyes and asked, "What sweetheart?" No matter how much I dreaded hearing her answer, I asked, "ma, where is Frank?"

I could see that the shock of those words wiped the loving smile from her face, replacing it with a puzzled expression.

"Michael, why ask such a question? Didn't everyone think Frank ran off with that Hilda woman years ago"?

"That story is impossible now, ma."

"Why is it impossible Michael?"

"It's impossible, because knowing Hilda; she would never have run off with a man that was lacking a peepka."

I could see my statement that Hilda would never run off with a man without a peepka didn't seem to sink in. There wasn't any change in her facial expression, so I knew I had to relate the whole story of what happened in the cellar. I told her about Diabel's surprise attack and how I finally got rid of him for good. I went on to explain that during the scuffle, I bumped into the island shelves and knocked down a jar of pickles that was marked for County Fare only. Hearing that, she immediately stood up and with the words, "Oh my God" darted toward the cellar door.

"Wait ma, there's no need to go and check the jar. It's the one with Frank's pickled peepka." When she heard me say Frank's peepka, she realized it was not a long dark secret anymore.

She slowly turned and came back into the kitchen. Without saying a word, she sat at the kitchen table, laid her head face down on her folded arms and released a loud mournful scream. I watched her body shake with deep uncontrollable sobbing and fought the urge to go over and console her. I thought it best to let her have a good cry to release the pressure harbored for so many years. With tear-stained eyes, I watched my ma in her terrible agony and wondered if my world would ever be the same again. What was even worse, would my feelings for her ever be the same. A mother I thought was incapable of doing such a heinous act. I couldn't believe this woman at the kitchen table, shedding those tears, was the same person who dedicated her life raising me. There was only one-way of knowing how this bizarre thing happened and the answer had to come from her.

I waited until her crying subsided then asked, "ma are you capable of telling me what this is all about, or do you want to rest for awhile?" She raised her head and with her apron wiped her tears. I could see dark rings had formed around her eyes, adding years to her features. With a voice that was very weak and shaking she said, "No Michael, I've got to get it off my chest before Marvin comes home. I hope you will somehow find it within your heart to forgive me. I've prayed every day since it happened, asking God for his forgiveness." She went on to say it took place the weekend I was at the Army camp in Indianapolis. The following is what I remember as she related her tragic experience.

She said, "I was in the kitchen preparing pickles for canning, when Frank came slamming through the door. He was yelling and cursing as he usually did when he had been drinking heavily. Friday was payday and he must have hit every bar on Franklin Street. He was mad at me for not having supper on the table when he got home. I told him the food was ready hours ago and it would only take a few minutes to warm it up. He just kept shouting and spitting on the back of my neck, as he pushed against me. He must have recently vomited, because his sour breath was unbearable. I had never seen him quite that wild before, Michael. I kept telling him to go lay down and I would feed him later. That only made him angrier, because as you know, he never liked me giving him orders. I tried to keep him away with a nudge of my elbow, but he came right back crowding me even more. It got to the point where I was hardly able to move at all. I thought of pushing him away, but remembered that the one time I did, he hit me so hard it took months for the bruising to clear up. I also tried to duck out from under his arms, but his elbows kept pinning me in. There wasn't any way of escaping. My only hope was that Frank felt like throwing up again and had the decency to use the toilet and not me. I got to the point where I just had to make some kind of a move. He began yelling even louder, about how your grandfather tricked him into marrying me. He said your old man lied about all the money he would give me to buy a tug of my own. The only thing I got out of the deal he screamed was, "A SISSY FOR A SON AND A GOD DAMN SHOE-STRING WIFE." When I heard him call me, a Shoestring wife, I wheeled around and with both hands shoved him as hard as I could. He staggered backwards against the kitchen wall. I quickly turned, covering my head with my arms and waited for the beating I was sure to get. I stayed cowering over the kitchen table, but Frank's punishment wasn't coming. When I peeked under my arm to check, I saw his back was against the wall and staring wide-eyed in startled disbelief. I was about to tell him I was sorry for shoving him so hard, when he began sliding down towards the kitchen floor. I rushed to stop his fall and when I put my hands up on his chest, to my horror, I felt the handle of the 'sword-breaker' knife. It was sticking out from the area of Frank's heart. The shock of seeing that handle in his chest, made me so weak, I didn't have the strength to hold him up. All I could do was watch his body as it slid down the wall into a sitting position, where it rolled over face down on the knife. Oh how I wished he hadn't shouted those words.

When he called me a Shoestring wife, Michael, something snapped inside and I lost all control. In my anger, I must have forgotten I had the knife in my hand.

The next thing I remember was leaning over Frank and feeling for a pulse. When I didn't find one, I knew the blade had entered his heart and he died instantly. It took a while for my head to clear and decide what to do. I realized I had to inform the police and call a Priest. On my way to the phone, other thoughts started crossing my mind… what if the police didn't believe it was just an accident and I stabbed him in a rage of jealousy. It would be easy for them to find out he had been seeing other women. I also realized there was a chance of going to prison or even being executed. I thought about you, without a mother, and living with all the shame, would be a terrible burden the rest of your life. I always believed in the saying, 'sometimes you have to do things to survive,' but how was I ever going to survive this. I knelt over Frank's body for what seemed an eternity, when suddenly the words… 'THIS TIME THE TIP-- NEXT TIME <u>ALL</u> OF IT,' entered my head. I remembered they were the words on the warning note that was pinned to Frank's shirt, the night the police found him lying against the cemetery fence. I couldn't stop wishing they had killed him then. It was because of that note, I got the idea to make it look like whoever it was that wrote it, followed through with the warning and this time cut off all of Frank's peecha. In the struggle that must have taken place, Frank was stabbed in the heart and just like before, left propped against the fence up the street from our house."

"To follow my plan, I had to remove the knife from Frank's chest. They could identify it as belonging to me. When I rolled him over on his back, I noticed he had bled very little. His heart stopped pumping as soon as the blade entered. When I tried to pull the knife out, I found I couldn't dislodge it. No matter how hard I pulled, it only raised his body off the floor. It seemed the knife caught on something inside his chest. It finally came to me that the notched side of the blade, the side that traps the sword of an enemy, had also trapped one of Frank's ribs. I even tried putting my foot on his chest for more leverage, but it still wouldn't budge. I was getting weak from all the tugging and pulling and had to stop and rest until I regained some of my strength. If I couldn't get that knife out, there was no way my plan would work. I then remembered your grandfather telling me that when a soldier trapped his opponent's sword, all he had to do was give the handle a quick turn and the enemy's sword would break right off. When I felt rested enough, I grabbed the handle with both hands and twisted as hard as I could.

When I heard a snapping dull thud in his chest, I knew then I could remove the knife. As I pulled it out, the tip of a rib stuck out."

"The next and most important thing I had to do was remove Frank's entire peecha. I was sure the police would remember the words in the note that threatened, 'THE NEXT TIME, <u>ALL</u> OF IT.' I had to follow exactly what it read. Time was running out. I dragged Frank's body out on the porch and waited until I was sure there wasn't any traffic coming. When I didn't see any headlights, I quickly dragged his body across the street and leaned it against the cemetery fence. I started to run back to the house when I realized if the police had any idea who it was that beat up Frank the first time, they could be blamed for this. What I was about to do Michael, was break the commandment and bear false witness against thy neighbor. I had to think of something else and fast."

"The thought of cremating him in Old Lucifer was one idea, but realizing that I would have to chop Frank into pieces ended that. I was in such panic; my mind wasn't functioning very well. I still didn't know where I was going to hide his body. Looking through a gap in the fence, I got the idea to bury him in the undeveloped section. His threatening statements of leaving someday and never coming back, would lead people to assume he had finally carried out his warning. It never entered my mind that the population of the county would grow to the point of needing more gravesites. I was looking at a big job, with little time to do it. I wondered if I had enough strength to dig a hole deep enough for a grave."

"I dragged his body through the gate and as I entered the cemetery grounds, saw one of the mistakes Dig-it Dugan had forgotten to fill in, the same one you and Mildred stumbled into, the night you played Ditch. I was relieved to see a hole half-dug. My next move was to get Frank's duffel bag and a shovel. I was about to run back to the house, when I saw a police car coming along Barker Avenue, shining his spotlight back and forth into the cemetery. I had to hide somewhere, so I pushed Frank down into the hole and laid over him hoping the mound of sand would be enough cover to block the policeman's view. As I waited, I wondered why he stopped and left the motor idling. I lifted my head and was startled to see him out of the squad car and heading up to the gate. I had all the reason to believe they would soon arrest me. As I waited, I heard the sound of the gate closing. What a relief to realize, in my haste I had forgotten to close it behind me. When the squad car finally drove away, I knew there wasn't time to dig the hole any deeper, because there was a chance the cop may become suspicious and return. I had to settle for the three feet that was available.

After a quick trip to get the things I needed, I removed all of Frank's clothing, except for his underwear and stuffed them into the duffel bag. I covered him with the sand from the mound, said a Hail Mary and Our Father and asked God to accept Frank into Heaven. I burned all of the clothing and duffel bag along with his shoes in Old Lucifer. The sight of smoke coming from a chimney in the fall of the year wouldn't seem out of the ordinary. When I started to clean up the kitchen I almost fainted at the sight of Frank's peecha lying on the kitchen table. I was in such panic getting rid of his body, I forgot all about taking it with me into the cemetery. There was no way for me to have the time or strength to go back and dig up the grave. I couldn't believe after all the work it took to hide his body; there was still part of it left."

"I got the idea of adding the peecha to the flames. Old Lucifer was red-hot by then and it would only take a few seconds for the peecha to explode into ashes. I picked it up and hurried to the stove with all the intentions of quickly opening the door and tossing it in. At that moment, I suddenly realized what I was doing. I had already gone too far by ending his life and depriving him of a Catholic burial. Instead, his body lies in an unblessed grave and I was taking it upon myself to send the last remains of him into the fires of hell. Dear God, what am I to do? I shouted. It was the first time I asked God for help and I was ashamed that I had forgotten the religious teachings of your grandmother Sophie. She taught me that if you ever need God's help, pray to him and ask for his divine guidance. She said God is watching and will always show you the way. She actually felt his presence many times. She even went so far as to say, she talked to God and heard his voice in return."

"I immediately dropped to my knees in front of Old Lucifer and started to pray. I said every prayer I knew and even said them aloud, shouting out to God to help me find an end to this awful thing that was happening. I was hoping for some heavenly revelation as to what I should do. I just couldn't believe God would forsake me at a time like this, but time was running out. I finally decided to go ahead, carry out my original plan, and accept any religious penalty. I held the peecha in my right hand and with my left hand quickly opened the fire door to throw it in."

"Then suddenly a very strange thing happened, Michael. When I opened the door to toss in the peecha, a paralysis took over the right side of my body. I could not lift my right arm. It just hung by my side and no matter how hard I tried I couldn't raise it. The door was so hot it was burning my fingers and I had to slam it shut. When I did, the paralysis left my right arm and the peecha dropped to the floor. I couldn't understand what was happening until I realized I was engulfed in a powerful magnetic force. It is hard to relate to you, Michael, but it affected me tremendously. I believed I was in the presence of God's aura. Yes, I was convinced it was God. The Lord stopped me from throwing Frank's peecha into the fire. I said, Dear God, if you do not want me to destroy it, then what should I do with it?"

"I couldn't believe that I actually spoke out loud expecting to hear his voice in return. I assured God that I understood I was not to destroy Frank's last remains, but then what was his reason for saving it? There weren't any words spoken and I could feel the strange magnetism had completely left my body. I knew then, God was gone. I picked up Frank's peecha and went back into the kitchen."

"I firmly believed God left it up to me to know what I had to do. I had already said prayers over Frank's body before I left the grave. What was so important about saving a peecha? It took awhile before I recalled somewhere in my religious teachings, that it is best to have a Priest, not me, saying the prayers over a deceased body. I thought maybe God wanted me to save the only flesh left of Frank, so that a priest would have part of his body when giving his blessing. Then I thought if that was what God wanted me to do, how was I to ask a priest to perform the ritual, without him notifying the authorities, which he would be obligated to do, so I had to stop that plan. I thought of putting it in the freezer compartment of the refrigerator, but they could discover it there."

"I had just about given up any sign from heaven, when I realized my eyes were staring at a jar of pickles. Lo and behold, was that God's answer? Was I to preserve it in a pickle jar? If pickles can last for years, maybe a part of a human being could. Therefore, I stuffed it in a jar with the label, FOR COUNTY FARE ONLY. I miss-spelled the word FAIR, to warn me it had Frank's peecha in it. I know it sounds very odd, Michael, but somehow it made me feel God would know how sorry I was and that I followed his divine guidance."

"But ma, it was an accident. You didn't plan on killing Frank, it was just a freak accident. Things like that do happen."

"I know, Michael, but there was a chance the authorities would not believe me and I'd be found guilty of murder. The thought of you living in shame the rest of your life, brought on by your mother would be more than I could bear. I had to think of some way things could remain the same and people would think Frank had merely run away for good."

"Now that you know what happened, you must inform the authorities." I stopped her from saying anything more by shouting, "No ma, I don't want to do that! I'll keep your secret and throw the peepka out in the garbage along with Diabel's carcass."

"You can't do that either, Michael, because then you'll be hiding evidence and be just as guilty as I am."

"You are only guilty of being part of a tragedy, not murder," I reminded her.

"I know Michael, but I don't want you to be part of anything I did. You are innocent and I want you to stay completely out of the picture. You'll have to tell the whole truth about everything."

She then suggested that we both try to get some sleep and the next morning I could put Frank's remains in a jar and relate to the detectives what she had just told me. I thought the suggestion of waiting until morning was a good idea. It was getting very late and exhaustion had weakened both of us. When I left to go upstairs, I saw her kneeling by the bed with her rosary. If she was praying for salvation, maybe I should pray for the wisdom to understand her episode with Frank's peepka. Her believing it was the presence of God who stopped her from destroying it and that she should save it for a Priest to pray over, was bordering on severe psychosis. The more I thought about it, the more I saw the correlation between my ma and Grandma Sophie. They both were very religious, claiming God had visited them and just like my grandmother, my ma too suffered with splitting headaches. It was only because of my Aunt Helen's persistence to check further, that they discovered a brain tumor that led to their mother's death.

My next thought caused me to sit right up in bed… is it possible that my ma was also suffering from a tumor. Could all the frustrating years of the tragedy put pressure on her brain? I made a mental note to ask Aunt Helen to help me talk my ma into seeing a doctor. Back then, they could x-ray bones, but not like the amazing equipment of today, show the inside of a brain. I didn't know how a doctor could determine a tumor existed, but we had to consider the possibility.

I was so engrossed in the fear that my ma may be a very sick woman that I forgot all about coming up with a reason she should let me keep her secret. I kept tossing and turning, racking my brain, but I couldn't get my creative juices flowing. It wasn't until I saw the first light of dawn approaching; that I came up with what I thought was a sound logical reason. I planned to tell her I couldn't go through life knowing I was the son that ratted on his mother. For me to live with that guilt, would destroy any chance of ever having a happy life. I would remind her that the police already filed the case away and would not pursue it any further. They should never send her to prison for a crime that was not a crime... but merely an accident.

I was so excited that I could save my ma, who already suffered from the loss of her high school love, a badly arranged marriage to a whiskey drinking, skirt-chasing sailor and the struggle to raise me through those devastating depression years. The fact that she harbored the pressure of knowing who was in the cemetery all those years should have been punishment enough.

I finally fell asleep from sheer mental exhaustion, only to awake later by a weird nightmare. It was a macabre picture of me dressed as a Priest. I saw myself standing by a fast moving conveyer belt, frantically trying to keep up with administering the last rites to an endless line of Polish peepka's.

Chapter 57

When I awoke the next morning, I found I had slept longer than usual. It was well past ten o'clock and Marvin would soon be home. I couldn't wait to tell my ma how important it was to let me keep her secret. I had to make her understand if I turned her in, how it would affect the rest of my life.

While I was patting myself on the back for my great idea, reality hit me like a ton of bricks. I sent my good friend Stash off to California, searching for someone who never even left the neighborhood. What a surprise ending for my movie 'Stash.' It again proves that truth is stranger than fiction. I couldn't believe at this devastating time of my life, I could be thinking of writing my movie, but the story was there and I just couldn't turn off my thoughts.

If Frank wasn't the one that Hilda used in the robbery, then who could it be? If the plan was to woo Stash into marriage and discover the hiding place of the Wolinski fortune, she had to have an accomplice, but whom? It couldn't have been one of the guys she had been auditioning in the cemetery, because they came later. (No pun intended.)

She was beautiful, but I don't think cunning enough to construct that plan on her own. Thinking along those lines, I remembered that one of his bootlegging suppliers introduced Hilda to Stash. They called him "Cap"; I think that was short for Captain. He made dark-of-night deliveries, to docks along the south shore of Lake Michigan for Al Capone. I was quite sure "Cap" was Hilda's mysterious accomplice. His criminal mind dreamed up the whole scam and the one who helped move Snowflake and Curly's headstone. It was Al Capone's supplier that left Hilda's sex ravaged body on the bed and ran off with the money.

Then to carry on with the scenario, Stash must have heard that someone on the docks in San Diego was flaunting his riches and discovered it was the guy who first brought Hilda to the tavern... the ex-sailor, Cap. What happened to him and Stash on that exploding yacht, and how much money was in the Wolinski treasure, will have to wait until the movie... Stash. I had to do things that were more important that morning.

I immediately headed for the cellar to remove the evidence and for the first time, started down the steps without the fear of that damn rat. I could still feel his claws digging into my flesh, as I pulled him away from my face. When I reached the area where the struggle took place, I carefully stepped around the scattered pickles on the floor. When I reached down for Frank's peepka, it wasn't there. I thought maybe I couldn't see it because of the dim lighting, so I grabbed a flashlight off the ledge of the stairs and used it to scan the floor. It wasn't in the area where I left it, so I started looking under the island shelves, thinking I might have kicked it under there. I couldn't believe something so soft and mushy could roll. I finally gave up my search, hoping my ma had already come down to get it.

Before going back up, I thought I might as well get Diabel's carcass too. I wanted to grab him by his long tail and give him a few more whacks against the wall, for good measure. I changed my mind knowing that my ma wouldn't like me treating any animal that way, even if it was dead. I shined my light back and forth along the base of the wall several times and didn't see any sign of him. I even checked the wall to see if the carcass stuck there, but it wasn't there either. Did my ma take the peepka and the rat, or did the rat take the peepka? I couldn't believe that after what I did to Diabel, he could still be someplace dining on Frank's pickled peepka. I was desperately hoping that it was my ma who returned it, because if it wasn't, then that damn Norwegian rodent is indestructible.

It was getting close to the time Marvin would be getting off the bus, so I had to hurry to convince my ma that she had to let me share her secret. As I passed by her bedroom, I noticed how neatly the room looked with the bed made. She often said when an angel came to get her; she wouldn't want it to be in an untidy place. At the time, I didn't have any idea of her whereabouts, but knew she always left a message on the refrigerator so that's where I headed. As I approached, I saw the note.

My dear beloved Michael.

I am sorry for what I am about to do, but I feel it best to punish myself for what I have done. To go on now, would only bring you more hardship. You have grown into the kind of man your father Martin would have wanted. You have so many of the characteristics he had and all the handsome features too. Marvin is a good man and I am sure he will be there for you the rest of the way. What I am about to do is against one of God's laws. I have been living a long time in a sinful marriage and I must put an end to it. I always felt the closest to God when I was in my garden, so that is where you will find me, as I break the fifth commandment. You know what I told you to do with that ugly thing in the pickle jar.

I love you with all my heart

your ma

Chapter 58

Fifth commandment? FIFTH COMMANDMENT! That's, *thou shalt not kill*... What was my ma going to kill? She certainly wasn't planning on a chicken or duck. I ran as fast as I could through the kitchen and out the back door and as I turned to go under the arbor, I was stopped in my tracks by the horrifying sight of her hanging by the neck. It left me so stunned I couldn't move, but just stood watching her limp little body slowly swaying and twisting.

The next thing I knew, my arms were around her waist as I tried to ease the strain on her neck. I could tell that all life had left her and that she must have been hanging like that for quite some time. A sudden shame came over me as I realized I couldn't remember the last time I held her in my arms. It was a gut-wrenching feeling knowing that all the hugging I would do now, would be much too late.

The sound of Marvin's voice startled me as he shouted, *"MY GOD, MICHAEL, WHAT HAPPENED?"* He was at the entrance of the arbor holding his hands to his head in disbelief at what he was seeing. *"MARVIN"* I cried, *"SHE HUNG HERSELF... MY MA HUNG HERSELF! IF ONLY SHE HAD WAITED TO HEAR MY ANSWER TO HER PROBLEM, SHE WOULDN'T HAVE HAD TO TAKE THIS WAY OUT!"*

"Michael, what do you mean she didn't have to do this? What did she tell you that would make her want to take her own life?" I knew I better not say anything more. If I did, Marvin would know all about her secret, a secret that from now on I alone must keep.

When I started to pick up the over-turned ladder to cut her down,

Marvin shouted, "*MY GOD, MICHAEL, WHAT ARE YOU GOING TO DO?*"

"I can't stand seeing her neck stretched like that, so I'm going to take her down." He stood up, raised his hands and with a stern voice said, "No Michael, we must leave everything the way you found it. You should not remove her until the police have a chance to check everything to prove that she did this to herself. I know it looks terrible, but she can't feel pain anymore."

I asked him if he would call the station, because I was feeling sick to my stomach and my head was about to explode. He helped me to the living room couch, where I must have fainted.

When I came to, he was wiping my forehead with a cool damp cloth. With urgency in his voice he said, "I hope you're feeling better now, because we have to get our stories straight before the police arrive." I informed him I was still feeling a little weak and dizzy, but thought I would be able to talk to the police.

"Well first of all, Michael, how did you get those scratches on your face? Did your mother do that?"

"No, Marvin, I got clawed by Diabel. You didn't get rid of the rat by smoking him out."

"Well, I'll try something else then," he followed.

"I don't know if you'll have to, Marvin. I smashed him against the cellar wall."

"Well then, Michael, what did you mean when you said you had a plan for her problem?" Somehow, I knew that it was going to be his first question and I didn't have any idea how I would answer without divulging the secret. There comes a time in everyone's life when a lie can save many unnecessary hardships and I was about to tell one. I came up with a story that was partly false. I struggled with this idea in my head before, but I wasn't sure my ma would ever go along with it.

I told Marvin I had a plan to ask Stash if he would loan me some money, so you and I could take a trip down to Mexico. We would find some little fishing village where the police captain was acceptable to under-the-table money. All he would have to do was falsify a few papers. The document would be a certified death certificate signed by the captain. It would state that they found the remains of a man's body in a burned down casa and his only identification was in the glove compartment of his car. We would then attach an autographed picture of Frank to the certificate to prove to the church that Frank is deceased; that way you and ma could have a Catholic wedding."

"Damn it, Michael that was a great idea. I wish you had told me about it. I certainly would have helped you carry it out. Personally though, I believe Frank must be dead and buried somewhere a long time ago." If Marvin had only known how right he was...somewhere was right across the street.

I was proud of myself for coming up with a quick explanation, but I knew I still had a bigger problem. How would I explain the message she left on the refrigerator? Marvin would certainly show it to the police, because it was a suicide note, which would exonerate us in any part of her death. I thought about destroying it, but he would question its disappearance.

With their high-pitched sirens blaring and brakes squealing to a sudden stop, the overreacting police force was back once again at our house. You would think they had cornered an escaped convict from our state prison. This, of course, brought the neighbors running over to see all the excitement. They immediately started roping off the area and it didn't take long before another police car came screeching up, with none other than his highness, Herr Rudolf Von Krueger... the Bulldog.

It is a documented fact that some people are born naturals at their chosen profession and the Bulldog was a perfect example. From the first day he came to our house, he somehow instinctively felt that here was where he could find the answer for the  mysterious skeleton. His relentless belief that my ma and Marvin had something to do with it was uncanny. I must admit, when I saw him get out of the squad car, a belated pang of admiration engulfed me. Krueger looked so excited to be back to the place where his nose originally smelled a rat and it wasn't Diabel either. He was in such a hurry to get out of the car; it knocked his derby off, revealing a lot more baldness than before. Right behind him was his assistant, Ellery, with his notebook and pencil in hand. The first thing Krueger did was order me and Marvin to go into the house, to question us later. We had no idea what kind of police work was taking place out in the garden. All we could do was sit there, sweating out the answers to the questions, the Bulldog was surely going to throw at us.

It seemed like an eternity before Krueger entered the living room. What started out as a full cigar was now just a butt stuck in the right corner of his mouth. I think if the doctors told him he had to quit smoking, they would have to remove the cigar butt...surgically.

He began his questioning with, "Who was the one that found her and why would she want to commit suicide?" The stub was now in the left corner and I swear I never saw him change it. Why it drew my attention at a time like that, I will never know. I thought that maybe it was one of his mesmerizing tricks.

I told him how I discovered her and thought I knew the reason she did it. I reminded him about the disappearance of her run-a-way husband Frank. I went on to explain her standings in the Polish church and that she was committing adultery in her new marriage. It also made her situation more difficult, because she couldn't confess her sin and receive absolution, which was devastating for my religious mother. Believing things would never change; she decided the only way out was to stop living.

I kept the other details to myself. The less I said the better. He asked if we had seen any change in her behavior lately. Marvin and I both agreed that we hadn't. All the while Krueger was throwing those questions at us, I noticed Ellery had his pencil poised over his notebook, anxiously waiting to record important information. Krueger would constantly turn to him and ask..."Did you get that kid?" Ellery would quickly say in return, "You bettcha, Boss." I got the feeling that the Bulldog must have eaten his ass out for not writing about those three missing men. After Krueger had all the information he wanted at the time, he stood up, switched his cigar butt and said, "I'll be back at a later date to follow up on that note your mother left you."

That note was the next big problem facing me. How would I explain the statement: "you know what to do with that ugly thing you found in the pickle jar."

The reason Krueger kept the interview short, was that he was running late for a planned fishing trip with some of the guys in the office. I was also elated to find out the trip was for a whole week up in Canada. I felt sure with that much time; my creative mind could come up with an acceptable answer. I had to tell him what was in that jar and still protect my ma's secret. What made the situation more difficult was, I had to accomplish this without lying ...she told me never to lie.

Chapter 59

The words on that note about the ugly thing in the pickle jar were constantly on my mind. How was I going to come up with a meaning to that line that would protect my ma's secret? Detective Krueger was nobody's fool and my answer had to be a good one. The week was flying by and I could not believe I only had two days left until the Bulldog would be knocking on our door. I spent the last two nights praying for some idea that would work. Maybe because of my prayers, a bolt came 'out of the blue' and I had the answer. Why not state that ugly thing in the jar was something else and still not lie. I was so excited; I literally jumped out of my bed shouting, "COME ON KRUEGER, I'M READY FOR YA!"

The next day he called and asked if I would be home. I informed him that I would be, but Marvin is at the prison. He said that was okay, because I was the one he wanted to interview anyway. Fifteen minutes later, he and Ellery were at our front door.

When I led them into the living room, Krueger immediately pointed at the chair I was to sit on, while he chose the couch directly across. I could see Ellery was excited by the way his hands were trembling getting out his notebook and pencil. I am sure Krueger had chided him on the lack of information he records. The 'Bulldog', as I expected, brought out the note my ma had written. He started by asking, "What was meant by the line...you know what to do with that ugly thing you found in the pickle jar?" It seems it was important to her to remind you to do it."

"Oh yes, I do recall that line, Mr. Krueger.

"Well then son, what was the ugly thing in that pickle jar?"

Without any hesitation I said, a pickle. It was the first time I ever saw the cigar stop in the middle of his gaping mouth. It hung precariously on his bottom lip as his eyes bulged in surprised disbelief to my seemingly rude and flippant answer. His expression was that of a renowned detective from Chicago, who believed I was making a fool of him. With a quick backward flip of his head, he returned the stub back into the safety of his mouth and asked... "A pickle?"

Yes, I quickly followed, "an ugly looking one at that, Mr. Krueger."

With an agitated voice he said, "Well, what in God's name did she want you to do with it son?"

"I think she wanted me to save it to show you."

By this time, the Bulldog's face was red as a beet and the cigar stub was changing rapidly from one side of his mouth to the other. It reminded me of the carriage on a reporter's typewriter trying to make a deadline.

"Why in the hell would I want to see a damn pickle, kid?" I told him about Diabel's attack on my face and the broken jar of pickles.

"I may be nuts for doing this kid, but go ahead and show me that damn pickle."

"I'd like to Mr. Krueger, but the rat ran off with it."

"You mean to tell me that rats eat pickled pickles?"

"Well, Diabel did, Mr. Krueger."

He said, "I never heard of a pickle-eating Gerbil."

"Oh Diabel wasn't a pet that lies on your lap and lets you tickle its belly, but boy did he love pickles." I swear I could see steam coming out of the Bulldog's ears as he started to take his frustration out on Ellery. Stomping his foot on the floor, he shouted, "FOR GOD'S SAKE, KID, DON'T JUST SIT THERE WITH YOUR MOUTH HANGING OPEN, WRITE SOMETHING DOWN," It startled his nephew, causing the pencil to flip up and settle on the brim of Krueger's derby. While Ellery searched frantically for his pencil, the 'Bulldog' kept his eyes glued on me. I could tell the wheels were rapidly turning in his analytical brain. He never uttered a word as his penetrating eyes kept traveling down at the note, then back up at me. I knew he was depending on that line to be the big clue in solving the case of the 'skeleton with the broken rib.' I sat nervously wondering how many times the Bulldog's watery eyes were going to keep looking up and down without saying a word.

What seemed like an eternity, Krueger finally looked over at Ellery, who was still looking for the pencil, turned and shrugged his massive shoulders and stood up to leave. My legs were trembling so violently I could hardly walk the detectives to the front door. Krueger turned and said, "Inform your father that we can't release your mother's body, until the coroner finishes his work. We will let you know when you can come and get it."

HE BOUGHT IT, OH MY GOD HE BOUGHT IT. Those wonderful words resounded in my head. My elation stopped when Krueger put his hands on my shoulders and with an expression of complete exhausted confusion asked..."You sure it was just some stinking pickle, son?" Without hesitating, I looked right back into those watering eyes and said, "Yes Mr. Krueger, a very...very...ugly pickle."

With a motion of his hand, he signaled Ellery and they both

walked out the door to the squad car. I watched the Bulldog as he stood pointing back at our house, shaking his head in complete disgust. It was obvious he wasn't satisfied with the results of the interview. I feared there was a good chance his doggedness (no pun intended) would make him come back with a new set of questions; one of which I wouldn't be able to skirt around. I could see he was still searching for other avenues, when he took Ellery's notebook and started thumbing through the pages. After franticly searching, he suddenly raised his arm and slammed the notebook to the ground. He also removed a freshly unwrapped cigar from his mouth and added it to the notebook. He started stomping on them with both feet, like a forest ranger putting out a neglected campfire. While going at it, the ill-fitted derby rolled off his head and proceeded to receive the same treatment the notebook and cigar were getting. Fearing for the derby, Ellery ran over to save it, and wondered how the lost pencil got way out there. In the meantime, Krueger picked up the flattened Shapo and sailed it like a Frisbee over the cemetery fence.

You can believe this or not, but it came to rest on the very same ground they discovered the skeleton with the broken rib.

I often wondered if the famous Detective ever knew the residents in the house across the street, duped him again. When I saw them finally driving away, I pressed my throbbing forehead against the cool glass pane of the door, raised my eyes to the heavens and said in a whisper... "Ma, if you can hear me, I didn't lie to the police, us kids always called a penis...a pickle.

Chapter 60

T he next morning I hurried out to where the two detectives were standing. I was very curious what notes Ellery had jotted down in his notebook. I was surprised to find that in spite of Krueger's Flamenco dance, all the pages had survived his hysterical onslaught. As I thumbed through the pages, it was hard to believe that with all the information given, he only entered one line. That line must have been the spark that ignited Krueger's explosive reaction. All Ellery wrote was A PET PACK RAT ATE AN UGLY PICKLED PICKLE.

I kept turning the pages in hopes of finding a following line like: IF A PET PACK-RAT ATE AN UGLY PICKLED PICKLE, HOW MANY UGLY PICKLED PICKLES WERE LEFT FOR A PET PACKRAT TO EAT? Obviously I didn't.

Chapter 61

The concern that my ma's soul would never enter God's heaven after judgment day left me devastated. My Aunt Helen feared I was on the verge of a nervous breakdown and I could see she was starting to take over the role of being a mother. She consulted the pastor at St. Stanislaus church informing him that I was in dire need of spiritual guidance. He promised he would come himself to explain the church's view on the subject of suicide. I was in fear that if his visit was anything like his sermons, I would be feeling a thousand times worse after he left. One time I told my ma that I hated the priest, because he wouldn't let her and Marvin have a church wedding. I also hated him for his sermons at High Mass. He was constantly telling the congregation they were all terrible sinners and if they didn't change their ways, would certainly see the fires of hell. I didn't like the fact he was including my mother and at times I felt like standing up and yelling, NOT MY MA, FATHER! As I think about it, he had ulterior motives for berating the parishioners so harshly. The collection baskets at any of his Mass' were always filled to the brim with monetary donations from sinners who were so shook up, they tried buying God's forgiveness. My ma told me I should never have hatred for anyone, but always try to understand. She would say, "Michael, the priest has to carry out the rules of the church and that is why he can't allow the wedding." I could understand not allowing the wedding, but why deprive her of going to confession or receive Holy Communion. I had my doubts if those were the rules of the Church or just his.

His visit came early on Saturday morning and to my amazement, it wasn't 'old fire and brimstone,' but a priest I had never seen before. He introduced himself as the new pastor at St. Stanislaus. He said the diocese needed to change some of the practices that went on in the parish. He never elaborated on what practices, but I had a good idea what some of them were.

Another thing that was surprising, he didn't wear the usual black suit and stiff white collar. He dressed somewhat sporty, with gray trousers, turtleneck and a sport jacket with embossed letters, N.D. I made a mental note to ask him later if that stood for Notre Dame, but in my excitement, I forgot. If he purposely planned to wear street clothes to make me feel more comfortable and less awed in his presence, it was working. For the first time I was seeing a priest as just an average human being.

He looked to be in his early forties and although he had some graying at the temples, you could see he had an athletic body under that sport jacket. I also noticed how tan he was, which led me to believe he spent a lot of his time outdoors. With his square-set jaw, deep blue eyes and a crop of black wavy hair, I was surprised he chose the priesthood.

At first, our conversations started out lightly about school and our favorite sports. Mine was baseball, his tennis. The more we talked the more relaxed and comfortable I became. It didn't take long and I was ready to talk about my ma's death. I said, "Father, I've been wondering if there was anything I could do here on earth to help her soul. One time I heard if a child entered the priesthood, his parents would go straight to heaven, no matter what sins they had committed. If I became a priest, would it release my ma's soul into Heaven on judgment day?"

"Well, Michael, there has been a great misunderstanding about God's judgment of people committing suicide. First, one cannot petition God. The church cannot preempt God's judgment in these matters. Purgatory cannot be permanent. It ceases at the last judgment, after which there is only Heaven or Hell. The Catholic Church teaches that suicide is wrong, but is not ready to say that every person that commits suicide is eternally separated from God. The catechism of the Catholic Church teaches us that everyone is responsible for the life God has given. God remains the sovereign master of life. We are obliged to accept life gratefully and preserve it for his honor and the salvation of our souls. We are only stewards, not owners of the life God has entrusted to us. It is not ours to dispose of. The catechism, on the other hand, also teaches that deep psychological disturbances, anguish, grave hardships and torturous suffering, can diminish the responsibility of the person committing suicide. You should not worry about the eternal salvation of your loving mother. By ways known to him alone, God can provide the opportunity for repentance. I would like you to know that the church prays for persons who have taken their own lives. Wisely, the Catholic Church in one of its Eucharistic prayers addresses God thusly ...and to all the dead whose faith is known to you alone. Only God knows the human heart well enough to make the awesome judgment about a person's salvation or damnation. So Michael, keep praying for your mother's soul. I am sure your understanding God is listening and by the way, did I understand she didn't have a funeral mass?

"No Father, the last pastor wouldn't allow it."

"I would be more than glad to say a funeral Mass for your mother," he offered. Funeral mass' are for the sake of the living as well as for the deceased. Not to allow a service for those who have committed suicide simply increases the survivor's heavy burden...which seems to be you, Michael."

He said he would set a date and inform the congregation well in advance. I couldn't help but wonder if anyone else would care to come to my ma's mass other than Marvin, Uncle Steve, Aunt Helen and me. If it turned out that way...so be it. She would have her funeral mass and the church would be praying for her salvation.

No one would ever realize how much better I felt after that visit by the new priest. My ma was right. You cannot alter the rules to suit individual cases.

They say that time is of the essence and timing is so important in life. If he had taken over a few weeks sooner, she would not have killed herself. She and Marvin could marry and be back in good standings with the church.

Oh, by the way, over a hundred people attended the mass. I saved you another question, didn't I?"

Chapter 62

I was completely overwhelmed by the amount of people that attended my ma's funeral mass. I never realized there was so many that knew and loved her. I am sure God heard all the prayers offered up for her soul's salvation and would consider it at Judgment Day. Her burial at Greenwood Cemetery was one of my most heart-wrenching events. The sight of her casket slowly lowered into that deep hole, has haunted me throughout my entire life. I can honestly say that for a grieving moment, I had the urge to throw myself on top of the casket and go down with her. As I watched, my thoughts reverted to the time she left me at my first day of school. That time however, she said she would return. I couldn't stop the tears that flooded down my cheeks, realizing this time; she was never to return.

Marvin and I agreed to wait a week or two before we discussed our plans. The ordeal we had just gone through had left us both mentally tired. When we finally decided to meet, he asked if I would want to come to Detroit with him. He said he had been corresponding with his cousin who owns a barbershop in the downtown area. His cousin said there was a great opportunity to start a chain of shops. He said we could sell the property and use the money to invest in his cousin's plan. He went on to say that if I liked the idea, he would teach me the barbering profession. "You see, Michael, there's going to be a great future in the hair grooming business and we would be getting in on the ground floor."

I did a lot of soul searching to Marvin's offer and decided that my ma would have advised me to take the one from my aunt and uncle about adopting me. Aunt Helen offered that statement in jest many times. Little did she know that someday in the future there would be that opportunity. I decided that living with a blood relative would be best and besides, Aunt Helen was a spittin' image of my ma. When I told Marvin of my decision, he seemed disappointed, but said he could understand my reasoning.

Selling the property wasn't as easy or profitable as we thought it would be. We ran into the same problems that the previous owner had. The house was just too close to the cemetery. We had to keep lowering the price until a developer finally bought the land. His plan was to tear down the house and build further back using the unfinished building that was to be my grandfather's general store. After signing all the legal papers, I let Marvin keep what little profit there was and wished him luck. The last I heard from him, he had remarried and as his cousin predicted the business had really taken off. They have since added a string of beauty salons managed by his new wife, Freda. I felt very happy for his good fortune, because no one deserved success more than he did.

My decision to live in Chicago with my new parents was the best choice I could have made. They say that everyone at sometime in their life comes to a fork in the road and choosing the right path isn't always the case. Helen and Steve made sure my choice was the right one. Thanks to them, I have a college degree in the profession I chose. I had to give up my prediction of becoming a major league pitcher. I got a big surprise when I tried out for the Cubs minor league team. Something destroyed my favorite pitch; the sudden rise of my fastball. No matter how hard I worked at it, it just wasn't there. I was told by the coaches that sometimes an arm can go permanently dead by throwing very hard without previously warming up. I couldn't remember when I did anything like that. I kept racking my brain until it finally dawned on me, that it might have happened when I hurled Diabel against the cellar wall. I threw him with all my might with a cold arm. To paraphrase a line used by James Cagney...YOU DIRTY RAT!

I picked the University of Chicago noted for its high scholastic standards. My residence would be near the college and I'd have a short drive. I would also be near my hometown and the greatest lake of all the great lakes... Lake Michigan.

The founder of the Botany department was Professor Henry Cowles who retired in 1934. He and his students conducted extensive field research in this region. His dedication to deciphering its bewildering diversity of plant life, led to the naming of a natural botanical preserve in his honor called, 'Cowles Bog.'

I obtained a Masters Degree in Agronomy, which has to do with plant growth. I knew my ma would be proud of her son, the horticulturist. They awarded me top student of the graduating class and I have her to thank for it. You see, while the other students were only fertilizing their growing projects with 'off the wall' products, I was adding... fish guts.

Except for the loss of my wife Mildred, I had a wonderful life all these years. She and the baby both died in delivery. You may be wondering if it was the same Mildred we played 'Ditch' with. To stop you from using up your one question, I must tell you it wasn't that Mildred. The name Mildred may have had some psychological effect in my choosing her for my bride. My ma would have been proud of me for marrying a good Catholic girl from a respectable family and staying clear from the clutches of a 'Shoestring.' As an afterthought, maybe she used the same perfume.

What I am about to tell you, came as a complete surprise. I was sitting in the stands watching the Yankees play a spring exhibition game, when a player came up and sat next to me. He immediately started asking me how I was getting along. I didn't have any idea why he wanted to know anything about me, until he said, "You know Michael, you were a few years ahead of me in school and my idol. I always hoped to be as good as you were, someday. I heard about your arm losing its big league pitches and seeing you up here, I wanted to let you know how great I thought you were." I told him I was thankful for his concern and wished the Yankees would win the next World Series. With that, he slapped me on the back and said, "I got to get back to the game, but the best of luck in the future."

A guy sitting a few rows in back said, "Hey, you didn't get his autograph."

I turned and told him, "I didn't intend to, he came up to talk to me. He went to the same school I did."

"I got his autograph yesterday," he proudly stated.

"Well, who in the hell is he?" You'll never understand the shock I got when he replied, "That's the only pitcher to ever pitch a perfect game in a World Series. His name is Don Larson."

I couldn't believe I was an idol to a famous athlete like him. I swear, on my mother's grave, it's the truth.

I am the only one left now. Uncle Steve died on one of his company's business trips. The jet crashed in bad weather on a mountaintop in Alaska. My Aunt Helen died a year after that with the same type of cancer Grandmother Sophie had back in Poland. There must be something in our family genes, because I too have an illness. I stopped going to doctors for physical check-ups and I am now battling prostate cancer and the doctor thinks it's too late for it to go into remission. My only hope is the Gypsy lady would be laughing her head off at that prognostication.

As I look back at my birth city, it is also sad to know, some things are no longer there. The amusement park closed in 1962. It was a suit filed by a city councilman, stating that the park board could not lease public grounds for private enterprise. Lakeview Amusement Park Company had already started removing rides and facilities from the park, even before the ruling was enforced. Although the Washington Amusement Park was given a twenty-year lease in 1965, the company and park board had disagreements, leading to liquidations. In 1972, the park didn't open. Gone were the rides, rollercoaster, Ferris wheel, the whip, penny arcade and even the shooting gallery. Another heartbreaking event was the dismantling of the Oasis Ballroom where we danced to big bands like "swing and sway with Sammy Kay," Glen Miller, Tommy and Jimmy Dorsey. If they were famous, we danced to them at the Oasis Ballroom.

However, you can still enjoy miles of shoreline, singing sands, beautiful beaches, sailing and great salmon fishing. There is also a zoo with a variety of wild animals. One of the biggest attractions was the monkeys on Monkey Island. It is surrounded by water and a cement wall provided for the viewing public. The island features gymnastic equipment for the frolicking primates. Feeding the monkeys was permitted and the animals learned that if they performed tricks on those bars and swings, people would throw food onto the island. It was hilarious seeing them showing off for their delicious treats. I don't think my ma ever visited Monkey Island. If she did, she would have barred me from ever going back. There was more open fornication going on than I ever saw on the most sexy Saturday night in Greenwood Cemetery. Needless to say, I went as often as I could. There were only two great zoos in the area, Chicago and ours.

There is a possibility my report on the demise of the family and the wonderful entertainment center has given you an emotional low. If so, I have made up a few anecdotes for comic relief.

Dig-it Dugan, after 30 years of cemetery gaiety, got promoted to night watchman at the fun-loving County Morgue.

Snort got a patent on a bicycle that when you pull up on the handlebars for a wheelie, it makes a neighing sound like a horse.

My 'Ditch' partner Mildred was top sales lady for a perfume company.

My pal, Blub was fired as a lifeguard for showing girls his 'pickle on a plate.'

'Bulldog' Krueger spent most of his retirement days at a little café called Grandma's Super Bowl. Her specialty was, Crew Protna... Duck Blood Soup. (Yug!)

No last name Ellery went on to teach public speaking for Dale Carnegie and used for a tongue exercise, "if a pet pack rat ate an ugly pickled pickle," how many etc...Four times without stopping.

The sex-crazed schoolteacher married and sent all her kids to a Catholic School.

The two renting Mississippi cowboys tried Hollywood and auditioned for the leads in 'Broke Back Mountain.'

Mr. Washington ended up coaching at a black Southern school. It all started when walking home from the cemetery, a kids basketball bounced out in front of him.

The rat, Diabel's intestines were so damaged, all he could digest were pickled pickles.

Remember... I told you I made them up, so if we happen to meet at a book signing, don't be like the kid about the squirrel and ask where you can buy one of Snort's bicycles.

Chapter 63

Before I end my story, I'd like to give a much deserved thanks to Helen and Steve for all their love and devotion. They were there for me when I was reaching manhood and facing the loss of a wonderful mother. Not only did they provide me with a college education, but also Steve was responsible for my being hired to head his company's landscaping project. They built their office building on a large acreage of land and needed a park-like setting. It was an enormous challenge for a kid who had just earned his Master's degree, but I was well prepared well for it. I remembered how beautiful Greenwood Cemetery looked with all those different types of pines. From my ma, I learned about growing beautiful flowers and arranging them so they grew to complement each other as they blossomed throughout the seasons.

The president of Steve's company was so pleased with the results they gave me the title of Park Superintendent and I held the job until I retired with a lucrative pension. I have willed my inheritance from my parents, to my parish for annexing a library room to our Catholic high school in my ma's name.

'Last but not least', I want to thank you for riding along with me for what may be my last trip. I feel relieved that I got the secret off my chest and left it with you. I'm sure you are wondering why after all these years, I finally revealed it. I have asked myself the same question many times. The only answer I can come up with is maybe a born writer cannot leave this earth when there is still a story to be told. If you don't want to bear the secret alone, tell a friend about this book.

Well, we are nearing the city limits and I will have to let you off here. I would not want you to see the name of the city on the billboard signs. As I said, there are no statutory limits of time on a murder case. Even if you did tell what you just learned, I could explain that it is only a novel and then again, maybe it's not, I will let you decide.

You have been an attentive listener, so I will state the clues: The city isn't a Michigan town - The Hoosier Slide - the Observation Tower - the Zoo – home of the Yankee pitcher Don Larson - the pier etc.

I hoped you enjoyed the story. Don't sweat the trip back because all you have to do is close the book and you'll find you really never left.

I've been anticipating all your questions so far, so I think I know what the next one is. You heard me say I will be visiting three graves and obviously, one would be my ma's in Greenwood cemetery and the second one, my grandfather's grave in St. Stanislaus Polish cemetery. What's the third one you ask? Well, in the book, "Mystery of MA's Ugly Pickle," it says… turn the page to find out.

About the Author

Martin Michael Neveroski (a.k.a. Marty Nevers) was born in 1923 in the Northern Indiana town of Michigan City. Blessed with a tremendous amount of athletic ability, he was captain of his high school basketball and baseball teams. After graduation, he entered the entertainment field. At eighteen, his crooning voice landed him a job on the radio station W.H.O.T. South Bend, Indiana. From there, he spent years singing with big bands at hotels in the Chicago area. Having the knack for comedy, he formed his own comedy band and performed in Las Vegas casinos. While working in Vegas, he spent his days off entertaining soldiers on maneuvers in Needles, California… in the fine tradition of Bob Hope.

While living in Minnesota he performed in Stillwater prison, the Shriners Children's Hospital and many other state hospitals. One of them was the Mayo clinic in Rochester where he performed for Ed Sullivan who was recovering from gall bladder surgery. Mr. Sullivan laughed so hard he popped his stitches and they made Marty stop. He was the only entertainer to visit Ed Sullivan in his hospital room.

His many years of performing in Minneapolis were filled with producing and hosting television shows including the popular Channel 9 program about high school activities called 9-TEENS.

Marty has written and professionally recorded sixty-nine songs available on four disks. He and his wife Carla still perform every chance they get.

Marty exposes his inner being in the "*Mystery of MA's Ugly Pickle*" but in all honesty, he just wants you to enjoy reading it.

FRASER AND NEVERS
DECIDING ON SALARY CUTS.
(Not part of show)

ARMOND FRASER

Armond's top instrument is trumpet, and he has a bachelor degree in music and dramatics (University of Minn.). One of the best stand-up comics in his own right, he has recorded many fast-selling records. In the duo-log bits, he plays straight man to Nevers. Armond sings, arranges, etc. Armond also does modeling and is featured on many T.V. commercials.

THE SYNC
IS PLUGGED

Okay, if acts that do pantomime to records are back in (and if you're a Fraser and Nevers fan, they never went out), then here's an Act for you!

MARTY NEVERS

Marty's most outstanding contributions to the act has to be his singing voice and facial contortions. He has written many of their duo-logs and has written and recorded his own tunes. Marty plays the comic in the act and also plays drums. He is sidelining in modeling work and is featured in many T.V. commercials with Armond and by himself.

"PANTOMIME"
Excerpts from the biggest selling records since advent of Rock and Roll.

"MOVING WEST"
(Duo-Log Sketch)

CPSIA information can be obtained at www.ICGtesting.com
Printed in the USA
BVOW021412130911

271047BV00005B/6/P